Y0-DDA-293

The Royal Dutch/Shell Group of Companies

Information Handbook
1972-3

Shell International Petroleum Company Limited, London

Foreword

The Information Handbook provides up-to-date facts and figures about the oil and petrochemical industries and the Royal Dutch/Shell Group of companies.

It has been designed for use in the normal course of business and to help Shell employees to answer questions, but its contents are not confidential. More detailed information about the various technical phases of the industry can be obtained from *The Petroleum Handbook*, published in 1966. Statistical material is available in chart form in the booklet *Oil in the World Economy* and deeper, more topical analyses of particular aspects of the industry are available in the *Shell Briefing Service*. There is also available a specialised *Chemicals Information Handbook*.

July 1972

In this publication the expression 'Group' is used for convenience to refer to those companies which are known as Royal Dutch/Shell Group companies or to one or more of such companies, as the context may require.

Contents

5 **Key facts and figures**

Organization (Shell)
7 Structure of the Royal Dutch/Shell Group of Companies
9 Managing Directors
13 Operating companies

Organization (World)
19 Some other oil and chemical companies

Finance
49 World
54 Shell

Exploration and production
60 World
65 Shell
74 Offshore

Natural gas
79 World
83 Shell

Marine
88 World
92 Shell

Pipelines
96 World
100 Shell

Refining
106 World
108 Shell

118 **Demand and supply pattern**

Markets and sales
125 World
127 Shell

Chemicals
130 World
134 Shell

Metals
143 World
145 Shell

Research
146 Shell

152 **Personnel**

154 **Useful conversions**

Key facts and figures

Finance

* The oil industry is very capital intensive. For US oil companies in 1970, the amount of capital invested per employee was about four and a half times the average for all US industry.
* In the 10 years from 1961 to 1970 the industry spent more than $156 500 million on capital and exploration projects, of which approximately one half was in the US. In 1970 alone the industry spent over $21 400 million, including $1 300 million for exploration.
* The First National City Bank of New York calculates that net income arising from Eastern Hemisphere operations of the seven major international groups of oil companies declined from around 78 cents per barrel in 1957 to under 33 cents per barrel in 1970.
* For the same group of companies, the rate of return on net assets has declined from 18·6% in 1957 to 11·2% in 1970.

Exploration and production

* In 1971 Shell companies had interests in oil and gas fields in 26 countries, producing an average of 4 526 000 b/d of crude and natural gas liquids.
* A land exploration well may cost more than £250 000 to drill; offshore drilling and development may cost three to four times more than a similar operation on land.
* Preliminary designs indicate that a permanent production platform for operation in 600 feet of water may cost £10 million.
* A major oil field can represent an investment of £300 million and it may take many years to reach pay-off.

Marine

* At 31 December 1971 Shell operating companies owned and managed 190 vessels (2000 dwt and over) aggregating 10·2 million dwt. This is 5·3% of the world tanker tonnage.

* By the end of 1971 Shell companies owned or chartered 45 ships of over 160 000 dwt.
* At 1 January 1972 Shell companies had 27 VLCCs on order for delivery between 1972–1976.

Pipelines

* In 1971 Shell companies acquired or participated in the building of 3,300 miles of pipeline in various parts of the world.
* Shell companies now own or have an interest in 51 650 miles of pipeline for crude oil, oil products and natural gas.

Refining

* At 31 December 1971 there were 74 refineries operated or under construction by Shell companies, or by companies in which there is a Shell interest.
* Shell refineries processed an average of 5 022 000 b/d of crude oil during 1971.
* During 1971 about 100 000 b/d extra capacity was added to Shell owned or partly owned refineries.
* For a complex refinery, capital costs are £400 – £640 per b/d of throughput capacity. For a 'simple' refinery, the range may lie between £250 and £400 per b/d.

Markets and sales

* Shell companies market in over 100 countries. In 1971 total sales of crude oil and products rose to 6 009 000 b/d from an average of 5 918 000 b/d in 1970.
* Outside North America Shell companies operate 1500 marketing installations, over 22 000 trucks, 20 000 rail tank wagons and about 450 000 dwt of coastal shipping.

Chemicals

* Shell companies' total net investment in chemicals exceeded £500 million by the end of 1971. In addition investment in joint ventures in which the Shell interest is 50% or less is approximately £50 million.
* Proceeds from chemicals represented $11\frac{1}{2}\%$ of Shell companies' total business in 1971.

Research

* Shell companies spent £53 million on research and related activities in 1971.

Organization (Shell)

Structure of the Royal Dutch/Shell Group of Companies

The Royal Dutch/Shell Group of Companies has grown out of an alliance made in 1907 between Royal Dutch Petroleum Company and The "Shell" Transport and Trading Company, Limited, by which the two companies agreed to merge their interests on a 60:40 basis respectively, while keeping their separate identities.

Today the title describes a group of companies the members of which are severally engaged in one or more phases of the oil, natural gas, chemical and metal businesses within various countries throughout the greater part of the world.

As Parent Companies, Royal Dutch and Shell Transport do not themselves directly engage in operational activities and are mainly vehicles for investment in the Group. They are public companies, one domiciled in the Netherlands, the other in the United Kingdom, and their relationship with the companies of the Group is illustrated on the next page.

Their merging of interests is expressed in joint ownership of two Holding Companies – Shell Petroleum NV (a Netherlands company) and The Shell Petroleum Company Limited (a United Kingdom company) – which directly or indirectly hold the shares (wholly or in part) of all other Group companies.

The conduct of operations calls for the concerted efforts of skilled people in the optimum deployment of oil, money and technology, within a sophisticated and flexible organization. At one end of the scale are the Holding Companies, concentrating on the disposition of capital, investment policy, returns and the appraisal of the results of investment. At the other lie the many Operating Companies, each preoccupied with running its business in its own economic, political and geographical environment.

The bridge between Operating Companies and Holding Companies is the Service Companies. There are four main

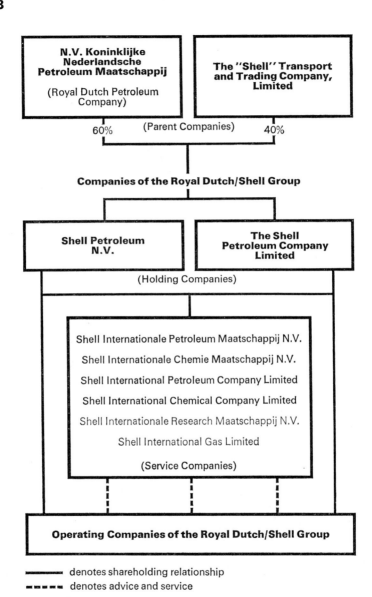

N.V. Koninklijke Nederlandsche Petroleum Maatschappij

(Royal Dutch Petroleum Company)

The "Shell" Transport and Trading Company, Limited

60%   (Parent Companies)   40%

Companies of the Royal Dutch/Shell Group

Shell Petroleum N.V.

The Shell Petroleum Company Limited

(Holding Companies)

Shell Internationale Petroleum Maatschappij N.V.

Shell Internationale Chemie Maatschappij N.V.

Shell International Petroleum Company Limited

Shell International Chemical Company Limited

Shell Internationale Research Maatschappij N.V.

Shell International Gas Limited

(Service Companies)

Operating Companies of the Royal Dutch/Shell Group

━━━━━ denotes shareholding relationship

▬ ▬ ▬ ▬ denotes advice and service

Service Companies – two for oil and two for chemicals (one of each in London and The Hague) – and also one each for research and natural gas. It is the business of these companies to provide advice and services to Group companies, to help balance varying aims and needs, and to undertake those functions that are most efficiently and economically supplied from some central point.

The individuals who are generally known as the Managing Directors of the Royal Dutch/Shell Group of Companies are members of the Presidium of the Board of Directors of Shell Petroleum NV and Managing Directors of The Shell Petroleum Company Limited. They are also Directors of Service Companies, by which they are appointed to a joint committee, known as the Committee of Managing Directors, which considers, develops and decides upon overall objectives and long-term plans to be recommended to the Operating Companies.

This brief description of the Royal Dutch/Shell Group of Companies is not exhaustive. Clearly, cases where the Group interest in a company or enterprise is less than 100% call for special consideration and, in some circumstances, for procedures different from those outlined above.

Managing Directors
Mr G. A. Wagner, CBE

Born 1916. Educated Leiden University (Law degree 1939). Before beginning Group service in 1946, held appointments in banking, town planning and civil affairs administration. Legal Department, Curaçao, 1947. Joined Compañía Shell de Venezuela, 1948. Subsequently held posts with Production Department, The Anglo-Saxon Petroleum Company Limited and with Eastern Area Management Department, The Hague. Assistant to Chief Representative in Djakarta, 1956. General Manager, Sumatra (Pladju), 1957. Manager of Planning Organization and Methods Department in Maracaibo; appointed Vice-President of Compañía Shell de Venezuela, 1959, and President, 1961. Appointed a Managing Director, Royal Dutch and Shell Petroleum, a Member of the Presidium of the Board of Directors of Shell Petroleum NV, a

Managing Director of SIPC, and a Director of SICC, SIPM, SICM and SIRM, 1964. Director, Shell International Gas, 1969. President of Royal Dutch, 1971. Chairman of the Committee of Managing Directors, SIPM, SIPC, SICC and Shell Oil, 1972. Also Director of several Group subsidiaries and associated companies.

Appointed an Honorary Commander of the Order of the British Empire, 1964. Order of Francisco de Miranda (Venezuela), 1965. Knight in the Order of the Netherlands Lion, 1969.

Mr F. S. McFadzean

Born 1915. Educated Glasgow University (Economics and Law degrees) and London School of Economics (Business Administration). Before beginning Group service in 1952 had considerable experience in British Civil Service. With the Board of Trade and later the Treasury and after the War worked for the Malayan Government – he was for a time a member of the Legislative and Executive Councils – and then for the Colonial Development Corporation in the Far East. Group service in various posts in the Service Companies and the Middle and Far East. Appointed Managing Director of Shell Petroleum, a Member of the Presidium of the Board of Directors of Shell Petroleum NV, a Managing Director of SIPC, and Director, Shell Transport, SICC, SIPM, SICM and SIRM, 1964. Managing Director, Shell Transport, 1971, Chairman 1972. Chairman, Shell Petroleum, and Vice-Chairman, Committee of Managing Directors, 1972. Chairman, Shell International Marine Limited 1966, Chairman Shell Canada, 1971. Director of PICA (Private Investment Co for Asia) 1969, Chairman Trade Policy Research Centre, 1971. Hon LL D, University of Strathclyde, 1970. Chairman of Steering Board of Strathclyde Division of the Scottish Business School.

Mr C. C. Pocock, CBE

Born 1920. Educated Oxford University (Classics and Philosophy). Began Group service in 1946. Worked in Venezuela, where District Superintendent in La Concepcion in 1955, and London, where he was appointed Head of Group Personnel Relations in 1959. From 1962 to 1964 was Vice-President of Compañía Shell de Venezuela, and from 1964 to 1967 President. In 1968 appointed Regional Co-ordinator East and Australasia. Director of Shell Petroleum NV and The Shell Petroleum Company Limited, 1967, and SIPC in 1968. A Managing Director of Shell Petroleum and SIPC, a Member of the Presidium of the Board of Directors of Shell Petroleum NV, and a Director of Shell Transport, SIPM, SICC, SICM and SIRM, 1970. Chairman of the Council of Industry for Management Education, 1972.

Commander of the Order of the British Empire, 1967.

Mr E. G. G. Werner

Born 1920. Educated Technological University of Delft (Chemical Engineering degree). Began Group service in 1945. Has worked at Amsterdam, where he became Associate Director of Research for Chemical Processes and Products in 1957, in London and The Hague and at Pernis Refinery. In the Chemicals Manufacturing Co-ordination, he became Head of Plastics, Resins and Elastomers Division in 1961, Head of Agricultural and Industrial Chemicals Division in 1963 and Co-ordinator in 1964. Director of Chemicals, 1967. Appointed a Director of SICM 1965; SICC, 1967; Shell Petroleum and Shell Petroleum NV, 1968; Chairman of SICM, 1968; a Managing Director of Royal Dutch and Shell Petroleum, a Member of the Presidium of the Board of Directors of Shell Petroleum NV, a Managing Director of SIPC and SICC and a Director of SIPM and SIRM, 1970.

Mr K. Swart

Born 1921. Educated Technological University of Delft (Chemical Engineering degree). Began Group service in 1948. After a period at Amsterdam, he was process design and start-up engineer at the Bombay, Geelong and Cardón Refineries. Assistant General Manager, Cardón Refinery, 1963; General Manager, Shell Curaçao, 1965; Director of Manufacturing and Supply, Compañia Shell de Venezuela, 1967. During 1968 and 1969 he was engaged on a special study assignment in the Central Offices. Appointed a Managing

Director of Royal Dutch and Shell Petroleum, a Member of the Presidium of the Board of Directors of Shell Petroleum NV, a Managing Director of SIPC and a Director of SICC, SIPM, SICM and SIRM, 1970.

Mr D. de Bruyne

Born 1920. Graduated in Economics, Nederlandsche Economische Hoogeschool, Rotterdam. Began Group service in 1945. In Finance until 1955 when he went to Indonesia, becoming Treasurer in 1957. Appointed Deputy Treasurer in London 1958. Finance Manager in The Hague, 1960. Finance Manager, Shell Italiana, 1962, and Executive Vice-President in 1964. Returned to London 1965 as Regional Co-ordinator (Oil) for Africa. General Manager, Deutsche Shell, 1968. Director of Finance, London, 1970. Appointed a Director of Shell Petroleum, Shell Petroleum NV and of SIPC 1970. Appointed a Director of Shell Transport, a Managing Director of Shell Petroleum and a Member of the Presidium of the Board of Directors of Shell Petroleum NV, a Managing Director, SIPC, and a Director, SICC, 1971.

Mr A. P. J. Bénard

Born 1922. Educated Ecole Polytechnique, Paris. Began Group service in 1946. Société des Pétroles Jupiter 1946–9 and Shell Petroleum 1949–50. On returning to France worked both in technical and marketing functions in Group companies in France, and in 1962 became President and Managing Director, Société pour l'Utilisation Rationnelle des Gaz. He was the Marketing Manager of Shell Française from 1964 to 1967 and President and Managing Director from 1967–70. In 1970 he was made Co-ordinator, Europe, Oil and Gas, and a Director of Shell Petroleum NV and The Shell Petroleum Company Limited. Appointed a Managing Director of Royal Dutch and Shell Petroleum and a Member of the Presidium of the Board of Directors of Shell Petroleum NV, a Managing Director of SIPC and a Director of SICC, SIPM, SICM and SIRM, 1971.

Awarded the Médaille de la Résistance in World War II. Chevalier de l'Ordre National du Mérite. Chevalier de la Légion d'Honneur 1971.

Operating companies

The main operations of the following companies are indicated by the letters against their names, the key to these letters appearing below.

Subsidiaries of these companies are, in general, not shown and some small operating companies have been omitted. The ownership percentages shown below include both direct and indirect holdings of ordinary shares in the companies named, in some cases rounded off to the nearest whole figure.

A	Agriculture
C	Chemicals
E	Exploration
Es	Engineering services for offshore operations
G	Geological studies
I	Industrial gas manufacturing and marketing
L	Liquefied petroleum gas marketing
M	Manufacturing
Mk	Marketing
MM	Mining and Metals
N	Natural gas
O	All main oil functions
P	Production
R	Research
T	Transportation

USA

	%	
Shell Oil Company	69	O,N,C
Asiatic Petroleum	100	Mk

Canada

	%	
Shell Canada	87	O,N,C
Canadian Fuel Marketers	100	Mk

Rest of Western Hemisphere

Caribbean

	%	
Conch International Methane (*Bahamas*)	40	N
Shell Bahamas	100	Mk
Coldgas Trading (*Bermuda*)	50	N,T
Shell Bermuda	100	Mk
Shell Antilles and Guianas	100	Mk
Refinería Dominicana	50	M
Shell (WI) (*Dominican Republic, Haiti, Jamaica and Panama*)	100	Mk
Shell des Antilles et de la Guyane Françaises	100	Mk
Antillaise d'Entreposage (*Martinique*)	25	Mk
Raffinerie des Antilles (*Martinique*)	24	M
Shell Curaçao	100	M
Shell Nederlandse Antillen	100	Mk
Pipelines of Puerto Rico	40	T
Shell (Puerto Rico)	100	Mk
Shell and Commonwealth Chemicals (*Puerto Rico*)	50	C
Shell Trinidad	100	P,M, Mk, N

Central America

	%	
Shell British Honduras	100	Mk
Shell Costa Rica	100	Mk

	%	
Refinería Acajutla (*El Salvador*)	35	M
Shell El Salvador	100	Mk
Refinería Petrolera de Guatemala-California	40	M
Guatemalteca Shell	100	Mk
Shell de Exploración Honduras	100	E
Shell Honduras	100	Mk
Distribuidora Shell de México	100	C
Shell Nicaragua	100	Mk

South America

	%	
Shell Argentina de Petróleo	100	O
Shell Brasil	100	Mk
Shell Chile Industrial Química	100	M
Shell Chile Distribuidora	100	Mk
Shell Cóndor (*Colombia*)	100	P
Shell Colombia	100	Mk
Ecuatoriana de Lubricantes	70	Mk
Shellgas (*Ecuador*)	50	L
Shell de Recherches et d'Exploitation de Guyane (*Fr Guiana*)	100	E
Guyana Shell	100	E
Shell Paraguay	100	Mk
Shell del Perú	100	Mk
Shell Suriname NV	100	E
Shell Suriname Verkoop	100	Mk
Shell Uruguay	100	Mk
Shell Sur del Lago (*Venezuela*)	100	E
Shell de Venezuela	100	O,N
Shell Química de Venezuela	100	C

Europe
Austria

	%	
Rohoel-Gewinnungs	50	P
Adria-Wien Pipeline	14½	T
Transalpine Oelleitung in Oesterreich	15	T
Shell Austria	100	Mk

Belgium

	%	
Belgian Shell	100	M,Mk
Distrigaz	16⅔	N
Bayer-Shell Isocyanates	50	C

Denmark

	%	
Shell Denmark	100	E
Dansk Shell	100	M,Mk

Finland

	%	
oy Shell ab	100	Mk

France

	%	
Shell Française	86	O
Française de Stockage Géologique	22	G,R
Shell-Rex	100	E
Pipe-Line du Jura	97	T
Pipe-Line Sud-Européen	19	T
Rhénane de Raffinage	80	M
Produits de l'Air	50	I
Utilisation Rationnelle des Gaz	100	L
Shell Chimie	100	C
Chimique de la Méditerranée	50	C

Gibraltar

	%	
Shell Gibraltar	100	Mk

Greece

	%	
Shell (Hellas)	100	Mk

Irish Republic

	%	
Irish Refining	24	M
Irish Shell and BP	60	Mk

Italy

	%	
Italiana per l'Oleodotto Transalpino	15	T
Shell Italiana	100	E,M Mk
Sub-Sea Oil Services	60	Es

Luxembourg

	%	
Shell Luxembourgeoise	100	Mk

	%	

Malta

| Malta Shell | 100 | E |
| Shell (Malta) | 100 | Mk |

Netherlands

Shell Delfstoffen Nederland	100	E
Nederlandse Aardolie Internationale	50	P,N
Riviertankscheepvaart	50	T
Rotterdam-Rijn Pijpleiding	40	T
Shell Tankers NV	100	T
Shell Nederland Raffinaderij	100	M
Shell Nederland Verkoop	100	Mk
Nederlandse Gasunie	25	N
Rotterdamse Polyolefinen	60	C
Shell Nederland Chemie	100	C
Verenigde Kunstmestfabrieken	40	C
Wavin	62	C
Shell Research NV	100	R
Billiton	99	MM

Norway

| Norske Shell | 100 | E,M, Mk |

Portugal

| Shell Portuguesa | 100 | Mk |

Spain

Shell Spanje	100	E
Española Shell	100	Mk
Industrias Químicas Asociadas	25	C

Sweden

| Koppartrans | 100 | M,Mk |
| Svenska Shell | 100 | Mk |

Switzerland

Oléoduc du Jura Neuchâtelois	49	T
Raffinerie de Cressier	75	M
Shell (Switzerland)	100	Mk

	%	

United Kingdom

Shell UK Exploration and Production	100	P
Shell International Marine	100	T
Shell Tankers (UK)	100	T
United Kingdom Oil Pipelines	36	T
Shell UK	100	M,N
IBE Ltd	100	M,Mk
Shell Composites	100	M,Mk
Shell-Mex and BP	60	Mk
Lubricants Producers	80	Mk
Shell Chemicals UK	100	C
Shellstar	100	C
Associated Octel	36⅔	M,Mk
Shell Research Ltd	100	R
Shell Aircraft	100	T

West Germany

Gewerkschaft Brigitta	50	P,N
Gewerkschaft Elwerath	50	P,M,N
Deutsche Shell Tanker	100	T
Deutsche Transalpine Oelleitung	15	T
Rhein-Donau Oelleitung	15	T
Rhein-Main Rohrleitungstransport	41	T
Deutsche Shell	100	M,Mk
Gewerkschaft Deurag-Nerag	50	M
Ruhrgas	15	N
Thyssengas	25	N
Deutsche Shell Chemie	100	C
Rheinische Olefinwerke	50	C

Africa

North Africa

Algérienne du Méthane Liquide	16	N
Shell Exploration (Libya)	100	E
Shell Exploratie en Productie (Libya)	100	P
Shell du Maroc	100	Mk
Shell de Tunisie	100	Mk

West and Equatorial Africa

Shell West Africa (Angola and Gambia)	100	Mk
Shell Camerounaise	100	E
Shell du Cameroun	100	Mk

	%	
Shell Centrafrique	100	Mk
Shell Congo	100	Mk
Shell Dahoméenne	100	E
Shell Gabon	100	P
Equatoriale de Raffinage (*Gabon*)	11	M
Gabonaise des Pétroles Shell	100	Mk
Shell Ghana	100	Mk
Shell Guinée	100	Mk
Shell Ivoirienne	100	E
Ivoirienne de Raffinage	15	M
Shell de l'Afrique Occidentale	100	Mk
Shell Mauritanienne	100	E
Shell-BP Nigeria	50	P,N
Nigerian Petroleum Refining	20	M
Shell Nigeria	100	Mk
Shell Sénégalaise	100	E
Africaine de Raffinage (*Senegal*)	12	M
Shell Sénégal	100	Mk
Sierra Leone Petroleum Refining	18	M
Shell Sierra Leone	100	Mk
Shell Tchad	100	Mk
Shell Zaïroise	100	E
Shell du Zaïre	100	Mk

East Africa

	%	
Pétroles de Djibouti	50	Mk
Shell Ethiopia	50	Mk
BP-Shell Kenya	50	E
East African Oil Refineries	$12\frac{3}{4}$	M
Kenya Shell	50	Mk
Shell Chemical Eastern Africa	100	C
Maritime de Madagascar	30	T
Malgache de Raffinage (*Malagasy Republic*)	$6\frac{1}{2}$	M
Shell de Madagascar et des Comores	50	Mk
Shell Chimie de l'Ocean Indien	100	C
Shell Co of the Islands (*Mauritius and Seychelles*)	50	Mk
Shell Moçambique	50	Mk
Shell de la Réunion	50	Mk
Shell and BP (Sudan)	50	M
Shell Sudan	50	Mk
Shell and BP Tanzania	25	Mk
Shell and BP Uganda	25	Mk
Shell and BP Zambia	25	Mk

Central and Southern Africa

	%	
Shell Botswana	50	Mk
Shell Lesotho	50	Mk
Shell (Malawi)	50	Mk
Shell Chemical Central Africa	100	C
Central African Refineries (*Rhodesia*)	$20\frac{3}{4}$	M
Shell Rhodesia	50	Mk
Shell Eksplorasie Suid-Afrika	100	E
Shell and BP South African Refineries	50	M
Shell South Africa	50	Mk
Shell Chemical South Africa	100	C
Shell Eksplorasie Suidwes-Afrika	100	E
Shell South West Africa	50	Mk
Shell Swaziland	50	Mk

Middle East

Abu Dhabi

	%	
Abu Dhabi Petroleum	$23\frac{3}{4}$	P

Cyprus

	%	
Cyprus Petroleum Refinery	$25\frac{1}{2}$	M
Shell Cyprus	50	Mk

Dubai

	%	
Shell Markets (Middle East)	100	Mk

Iran

	%	
Iranian Oil Exploration and Producing	14	P
Iranian Oil Refining	14	M
Shell Oil Iran	100	Mk
Naft Pars	$33\frac{1}{3}$	M,M
Shell Chemical Iran	$42\frac{1}{2}$	C
Iran Shellcott	$70\frac{1}{2}$	A

Iraq

	%	
Basrah Petroleum	$23\frac{3}{4}$	P
Iraq Petroleum	$23\frac{3}{4}$	P,T,M
Mosul Petroleum	$23\frac{3}{4}$	P

	%	

Kuwait

Kuwait Shell Petroleum Development	100	E

Lebanon

Shell Lebanon	50	Mk

Oman

Oman Shell	100	E
Petroleum Development (Oman)	85	P

Qatar

Qatar Petroleum	23¾	P
Shell Qatar	100	P

Turkey

Turkse Shell	100	P
Anadolu Tasfiyehanesi	27	M
Shell Turkey	100	Mk

Far East and Australasia

Brunei

Brunei Shell	100	P,N
Brunei LNG	45	N

Cambodia

Shell du Cambodge	100	Mk

Hong Kong

Shell Hong Kong	100	Mk

India

Burmah-Shell Refineries	50	M
Burmah-Shell India	50	Mk
National Organic Chemical Industries	33⅓	C

B

	%	

Indonesia

Djawa Shell	100	E
Kaltim Shell	100	E

Japan

Nishi Nihon	50	E
Shell Sempaku	100	T
Seibu Sekiyu	20	M
Showa Sekiyu	50	M,Mk
Showa Yokkaichi	50	M
Shell Sekiyu	100	Mk
Mitsubishi Yuka	27½	C
Shell Kagaku	100	C

Korea

Korea Shell	100	E
Kukdong Shell Oil	50	M,Mk
Kukdong Shell Petroleum	50	M,Mk

Laos

Shell du Laos	100	Mk

Malaysia

Sabah Shell	100	E
Sarawak Shell	100	P,M
Shell Refining (FOM)	75	M
Shell Malaysia	100	Mk
Shell Malaysia Trading	100	Mk
Shell Marketing Borneo	100	Mk

Pakistan

Pakistan Refinery	15	M
Pakistan Burmah Shell	24½	Mk
Burshane (Pakistan)	41	L

Philippines

Shell Philippines	75	M,Mk
Shell Chemical (Philippines)	40	C

Singapore

Shell Eastern Petroleum	100	M
Shell Singapore	100	Mk

	%	
Thailand		
Shell Thailand	100	Mk
Vietnam		
Shell Viet-Nam	100	Mk
Australia		
Shell Minerals Exploration (Australia)	100	E
Shell Development (Australia)	100	P
WAG Pipeline	33½	T
Shell Refining (Australia)	100	M
Shell Australia	100	T,Mk
Shell Chemical (Australia)	100	C
Western Australia Natural Gas	29	N

	%	
New Zealand		
BP Shell Aquitaine and Todd	25	E
BP Shell Todd (Canterbury) Services	25	E
Shell BP and Todd	37½	P,N
Shell and BP Pipeline Services	50	T
New Zealand Refining	17	M
Shell Oil New Zealand	100	Mk
Pacific Islands		
Shell (Pacific Islands)	100	Mk
Shell des Iles Françaises du Pacifique	100	Mk
Tonga		
Tonga Shell	100	E

Organization (World)

Some other oil and chemical companies

Abu Dhabi Marine Areas (ADMA)
Owned two-thirds by BP and one-third by CFP; produces from offshore Abu Dhabi – a pipeline connects the Zakum field to the loading and storage facilities on Das Island.

Abu Dhabi Petroleum Company
Owned 23·75% each by The Shell Petroleum Company Ltd, CFP, BP, and Near-East Development Corporation, and 5% by Participations and Explorations Corporation; produces onshore in Abu Dhabi.

Administración Nacional de Combustibles, Alcohol y Portland (ANCAP)
The Uruguayan state oil company, which holds a monopoly for crude-oil refining. Owns a refinery, storage and delivery plant at La Teja.

AGIP SpA
See Ente Nazionale Idrocarburi (ENI).

Algemene Kunstzijde Zout-Organon (AKZO)
Formed in 1969 by the merger of two Dutch companies, AKU NV, a producer of synthetic fibres and organic chemicals, and Koninklijke Zout-Organon (KZO) manufacturer of inorganic chemicals, pharmaceuticals, coatings, speciality chemicals and food products. AKZO now wholly owns Konam NV, a petrochemical manufacturer in the Netherlands. Fibres and chemicals are produced in the Netherlands, other West European countries, the USA and elsewhere.

Amerada Hess Corporation

In June 1969, Hess Oil and Chemical (petroleum refiner and marketer) was merged into Amerada. Amerada Hess operations are carried on through Amerada and Hess divisions. The corporation has active interests in Abu Dhabi, Argentina, Australia, Cameroun, Canada, Colombia, Ghana, Morocco, Togo, Trinidad and Tobago, Turkey, Venezuela and offshore the UK and Norway. In Libya, Shell Exploratie en Productie Mij (Libya) NV has an undivided half interest in Amerada's share in the Oasis concessions. Owns refineries at Port Reading, at Purvis and on St Croix, Virgin Islands. The corporation commenced a programme of exploration for uranium and other minerals early in 1967.

American Independent Oil Company (Aminoil)

Formerly owned by Phillips, Signal and several other US independent petroleum companies. Effective 1 September 1970 R J Reynolds Industries Inc became owner of the stock. The company has production and/or refining interests in the Kuwait/Saudi Arabia Neutral Zone, in Iran through its interest in Iranian Oil Participants (IOP) and in Rhodesia through its 15% participation in Central African Petroleum Refineries. Aminoil is also a participant in a consortium of three companies which, early in 1967, was granted a concession in Abu Dhabi. In January 1971 Aminoil obtained a 48·3% interest in a production sharing contract offshore south Sumatra. Aminoil is operator and initiated drilling activities in April 1971.

American Overseas Petroleum (Amoseas)

Owned jointly by Standard Oil Company of California and Texaco Inc. The company is involved in exploration and production activities in Indonesia and Libya.

Amoco

See Standard Oil Company (Indiana).

ANIC SpA

See Ente Nazionale Idrocarburi (ENI).

ANTAR
See Pétroles de l'Atlantique.

Aquitaine
See Société Nationale des Pétroles d'Aquitaine (SNPA).

Arabian American Oil Company (Aramco)
Owned 30% each by Standard Oil Company of California, Texaco Inc and Standard Oil Company (New Jersey) and 10% by Mobil Oil Corporation. Aramco produces, refines and markets in Saudi Arabia.

Arabian Oil Company (Arabia Sekiyu KK)
A Japanese company in which the governments of Saudi Arabia and Kuwait each hold a 10% participation. Explores and produces offshore in the Kuwait/Saudi Arabia Neutral Zone. Also operates the Khafji refinery which came on stream in 1968.

Aral AG
Marketer and distributor of petroleum products in West Germany and elsewhere in Europe; owned 28% each by Gelsenberg AG, Veba Chemie AG and Mobil Oil AG, 15% by Wintershall AG, and 1% by other private investors.

Arpet Petroleum
A wholly owned subsidiary of Atlantic Richfield. Explores and exploits hydrocarbons in the North Sea. The Arpet group holds 45·8% interest in the Hewett field operation. A gas sales contract was signed in early 1969 with the UK Gas Council.

Atlantic Richfield Company
An independent US company active in the production, refining, transportation and marketing of petroleum and allied products. Explores in a number of countries and through subsidiaries has interests in the UK and Dutch sectors of the North Sea. Obtains crude from the Gulf of Mexico, Venezuela, Colombia, Iran (through an interest in Iricon Agency) and Alaska, where it has a 48·5% interest in a producing field on the Kenai Peninsula and a 50% interest in the Kenai Pipe Line. Markets through subsidiaries in Brazil and the UK. Absorbed the Richfield Oil Corporation in 1966. In March 1969 Atlantic

Richfield and Sinclair Oil Corporation merged through an exchange of stock. Simultaneously with the merger with Sinclair, the company sold to BP Oil Corporation the Sinclair marketing properties and related assets in the south-eastern states, as well as the marketing properties of Sinclair in the north-eastern states of the US, including two refineries. The company holds a 28·08 % interest in Alyeska Pipeline Service Company.

Badische Anilin-und Soda-Fabrik AG (BASF)
One of the big three West German chemical companies, along with Hoechst and Bayer. Main product groups are plastics, coatings, synthetic fibre materials, agricultural chemicals, dyestuffs and auxiliaries. Manufacturing activities in West Germany are largely concentrated at Ludwigshafen-am-Rhein. Is a partner with Deutsche Shell in Rheinische Olefinwerke GmbH (ROW) at Wesseling and also in Compagnie Chimique de la Méditeranée (Cochimé) at Berre. BASF has recently constructed new plants at Antwerp and at other sites in Europe and has been particularly active in South America. In the US has merged its US subsidiaries, BASF Corporation and Wyandotte Chemical Corporation to form BASF Wyandotte Corporation. BASF holds over 95 % interest in Wintershall AG.

Bahrain Petroleum Company (Bapco)
One of the principal companies of the Caltex Group, owned by Standard Oil Company of California (50 %) and Texaco (50 %). Produces, refines and markets on Bahrain Island.

Basrah Petroleum Company
Owned by the same companies as Iraq Petroleum Company; produces in southern Iraq.

Belco Petroleum Company
US company chiefly concerned with the exploration, development and operation of natural gas and oil properties in Peru, the USA and Canada. Also has an interest in properties onshore and offshore Israel and onshore Italy and Sicily. In December 1968 the company issued 215 000 shares of its common stock in exchange for all the outstanding stock of

Sonneborn Associates Petroleum Corporation (SONAPCO) and the operating assets of Petroleum Transport and Trading Corporation. SONAPCO imports crude oil into Israel for processing by others and markets resulting petroleum products.

British Petroleum Chemicals International Ltd

Co-ordinates the chemical interests within the BP group. Though small in comparison with the world-wide Shell and Esso chemical interests, it has a prominent position in the UK chemical industry. In addition to its consolidated operations, it has large holdings in associated companies in France and West Germany, and smaller interests in companies in Australia, India, Kuwait and South Africa.

British Petroleum Company (BP)

A UK company engaged in all phases of the oil industry. Major shareholdings are held by the British Government (48·6%) and Burmah Oil Company (about 23% of ordinary shares).

BP has a 50% interest in Kuwait Oil Company, a 40% share in Iranian Oil Participants and a 23·75% interest in the Iraq Petroleum Company Ltd. It is in partnership with a Shell company in Nigerian production and also holds exploration concessions in the UK, Dutch and West German sectors of the North Sea. BP markets in Europe, Africa, Malaysia, Canada, Australia, and in the UK and Ireland through participation in Shell-Mex and BP and in parts of Africa through Consolidated Petroleum.

On 4 March 1969, assets purchased from Atlantic Richfield Company by the BP group were transferred to BP Oil Corporation. These assets comprise some 9700 retail outlets in 16 states in the USA, two refineries, together with a number of bulk plants, terminals and related transportation facilities. In 1969 the merger of Sohio and BP's subsidiary was approved and BP acquired 25% interest in Sohio which could increase to a maximum of 54%, depending on the level of production from BP's Alaskan acreage. *See* Standard Oil Company (Ohio).

The takeover of Alexander Duckham in 1970 leaves Duckham as a separate subsidiary within BP, retaining its identity.

Expansion of several refineries is being carried out notably at Grangemouth, where capacity will be doubled and the range of products widened.

BP Petroleum Development

A wholly owned subsidiary of BP engaged in petroleum exploration and development. Discovered gas in the UK sector of the North Sea during 1965 and began deliveries to the British Gas Council in July 1967.

Burmah Oil Company (BOC)

Owns about 23 % of British Petroleum Company's shares and has a 3·3 % interest in The "Shell" Transport and Trading Company. The group's present sources of crude oil and natural gas production are in India, Pakistan, Bangladesh, Australia, Canada, USA, Peru and Ecuador, in each of which countries it shares operating interests with other parties. The company also has exploration interests in these countries and in the North Sea. Companies of the Burmah group own a refinery at Digboi in Assam and two others in the UK and also have interests in refineries at Bombay, Karachi, Chittagong and in Ecuador. Markets in Assam, parts of Bangladesh and through Burmah-Shell in India and Pakistan Burmah Shell in Pakistan.

Caltex Petroleum Corporation

The name of California Texas Oil Corporation was changed to Caltex Petroleum Corporation on 1 January 1968. Caltex is owned equally by Standard Oil Company of California and Texaco, and is a supplier of petroleum and its products; provides general services for the Caltex group of companies; and holds interests in companies conducting exploration, producing, refining, marine transportation and marketing. The splitting of the Caltex assets in Europe between the two parents was finalised in May 1967, with Texaco emerging with the larger holding. Caltex holdings in France, Spain and Turkey, and its operations east of Suez, continue under joint ownership.

Chevron

Principal brand name of Standard Oil Company of California (Socal). Since 1965 has appeared in the name of several of Socal's subsidiaries in the Western Hemisphere and in the names of chemical affiliates in the Eastern Hemisphere. In May 1967 a new subsidiary of Socal, Chevron Oil Europe, took over some 50 % of the total operations of the former Caltex companies in 12 countries of Western Europe. (*See* Caltex).

Ciba-Geigy AG
Formed in 1970 as a result of a merger between the two main Swiss chemical firms, Ciba AG and J R Geigy SA. The combined product range covers dyes, pharmaceuticals, agricultural chemicals, plastics, photographic materials and consumer products. Following the merger, Ciba Corp, USA and Geigy Chemical Corp, USA were combined to form Ciba-Geigy Corporation and similar mergers have occurred in other countries including the UK. Has affiliates in 45 countries.

Cities Service Company
A US company owning securities of companies that operate in the natural resources fields. Company operates in countries in both hemispheres. Has a 25% interest in the Signal Oil group's concessions in the UK sector of the North Sea and holds one-seventh of the 50% interest held by a group of US companies drilling offshore Iran. Has fairly substantial chemical interests in USA.

Commonwealth Oil Refining Company (CORCO)
Incorporated in Puerto Rico in 1953, and is now one of the US's largest independent refiners, operating an oil refinery at Guayanilla Bay, near Ponce, Puerto Rico, and has contracts for the purchase of crude and the sale of refined products with major oil companies or their affiliates. Petrochemical interests include a wholly owned benzene plant and joint ventures with PPG Industries Inc (olefins), Hercules (raw materials for polyester fibre) and W R Grace (oxo-alcohols). SACCI – Shell and Commonwealth Chemicals Inc – is a joint venture with Royal Dutch/Shell at Peñuelas producing cyclohexane at a plant completed in 1967.

Compagnie Française de Raffinage (CFR)
Compagnie Française des Pétroles holds approximately 55% interest in this company, which operates refineries and markets in France, both on its own account and through Total. Has a 51% interest in Soc du Pipeline de la Raffinerie de Lorraine and also in Soc de la Raffinerie de Lorraine.

Compagnie Française des Pétroles (CFP)

An integrated French company in which the French Government has a 35% stock interest and 40% voting rights. The company owns 23·75% share in the Iraq Petroleum Company, Basrah Petroleum Company, Mosul Petroleum Company, Qatar Petroleum Company and Abu Dhabi Petroleum Company, 33·3% interest in Abu Dhabi Marine Areas, 50% in Dubai Marine Areas, 6% in Iranian Oil Participants and 10% in Petroleum Development (Oman). A subsidiary has been formed in Italy – Total Mineraria SpA – to search for and exploit hydrocarbons and other minerals. CFP has interests in offshore areas of Madagascar, South Africa, Angola, Labrador and Indonesia. CFP has a 30% interest in a refinery in South Africa which went on stream early 1971 and, with NIOC, will supply the refinery's crude oil. Markets in many European and African countries and in Australia (under the name of Total), where it merged with Boral to form Total Boral.

Compañía Arrendataria del Monopolio de Petróleos SA (Campsa)

The Spanish state marketing monopoly agency. Also holds interests in exploration concessions in Spain.

Compañía Española de Petróleos SA (Cepsa)

Spain's largest privately owned enterprise; it has concessions in Venezuela and exploration rights in Spain, Africa and Iran. Has a refinery in Tenerife, and a refinery and petrochemical plant at Algeciras.

Continental Oil Company (Conoco)

US independent with production in Libya, Venezuela and in Iran (through San Jacinto's interest in IOP). It also produces from offshore Dubai, has a widespread exploration programme in the Eastern Hemisphere and holds concessions in the UK, Dutch and Norwegian sectors of the North Sea. Recently Conoco USA (85% share) and Conoco Norway (15% share) have jointly set up an oil exploration company to drill in the North Sea. In the USA the company is exploring for uranium and has phosphate rock mining and processing operations. Owns and operates various refineries including one at Killingholme in the UK which began operations early in 1970.

Exploration, production and transportation activities in Canada are conducted through Hudson's Bay Oil and Gas Co, in which Conoco has a 54·9% interest. Also holds a 40% interest in Conch International Methane and the whole of the capital of Jet Petroleum, UK distributors. Has sizeable chemical interests in the USA and West Europe.

Corporación Venezolana del Petróleo (CVP)
A government company which explores, produces, refines and markets in Venezuela. It owns and operates a 25 000 b/d refinery at Morón and is planning to construct two new refineries.

Creole Petroleum Corporation
Owned 95·4% by Standard Oil Company (New Jersey) and the rest privately; operates as an integrated company in Venezuela and is an exporter of crude and refined products. It is the largest producing company in Venezuela.

Daikyo Oil Company
A Japanese company engaged in oil refining, marketing, importing and exporting of petroleum products. Daikyo is one of three Japanese companies which in 1967 were jointly awarded a 40-year concession offshore Abu Dhabi.

Dow Chemical Company
A US chemical company which produces a diversified line of basic organic and inorganic chemicals, plastics, pharmaceuticals, metals, agricultural chemicals, packaging and consumer products. Chemicals and metals between them account for about one half of total sales while plastics and packaging products account for a further one-third. The bulk of sales are made in the USA. However Dow has subsidiaries and associates in a number of West European countries, Australia and Latin America. Dow's largest plant in Europe is at Terneuzen in the Netherlands, while a large new complex is building up at Stade in West Germany.

Dubai Marine Areas Ltd
Owned 50% by CFP and 50% by Hispanoil; explores for and produces crude oil offshore Dubai.

E I Dupont de Nemours and Company

This US company is the largest concern in the world chemical industry. It is the largest producer of man-made fibres in the world (about a third of total sales) and also manufactures elastomers, plastics, pharmaceuticals, photographic products, paints, industrial films, industrial chemicals, biochemicals and explosives. In the USA it operates nearly 100 plants in 30 states and has about 100 research and development laboratories. In addition it has growing investments in subsidiaries and affiliates in Canada, Western Europe, Latin America and the Far East.

ELF (Essences et Lubrifiants de France)

See Entreprise de Recherches et d'Activités Pétrolières (ERAP).

Empresa Colombiana de Petróleos (ECOPETROL)

A state-owned company which produces, refines and markets in Colombia. Owns and operates the Barrancabermeja refinery.

Empresa Nacional del Petróleo (ENAP)

A state organization which carries out all exploration, production and refining in Chile. ENAP and the Chilean State Development Corporation each hold a half-interest in Petroquímica Chilena, formed in May 1966, to operate a petrochemical complex expected on stream by 1972.

Ente Nazionale Idrocarburi (ENI)

Established by the Italian State. Explores, produces, refines and markets in Italy and in Africa. Markets in a number of European countries and has a refinery in West Germany. The Zambian Government and ENI will have equal interest in a 1·1 million tons per annum refinery to be constructed in Ndola and scheduled for completion in 1972. ENI has production in Egypt, through International Egyptian Oil Company's 50% interest in Compagnie Orientale des Pétroles d'Egypte (COPE) and in Iran, through Société Irano-Italienne des Pétroles (SIRIP) which it owns jointly with National Iranian Oil Company (NIOC). It has concessions in several other areas but exploration is now directed mainly to the Adriatic continental shelf and the Alaskan North Slope. The principal operating, companies and share interests held by ENI are AGIP (84% –

oil exploration, production, marketing), ANIC (70·4% – refining, chemicals), and SNAM (100% – transport, distribution of natural gas). Subsidiary companies also operate in the fields of nuclear energy, chemical and mechanical engineering and textiles. In early 1969 ENI and IRI jointly acquired sizeable interests in Montecatini-Edison, Italy's largest chemical company.

Entreprise de Recherches et d'Activités Pétrolières (ERAP)
Essences et Lubrifiants de France (ELF)

A state-owned company formed to merge the undertakings of BRP (Bureau de Recherches de Pétrole) and RAP (Régie Autonome des Pétroles). Interested in all phases of the petroleum industry, directly or through affiliates in France and abroad. Exploration and production activities are carried out by wholly owned Soc Elf pour la Recherche et l'Exploitation des Hydrocarbures, refining and marketing by wholly owned Elf Union. In December 1971 the chemical interests of ELF/ERAP were associated with those of Total and Aquitaine in a new company ATO.

Esso

Brand name of Standard Oil Company (New Jersey); appears in the names of most of its operating subsidiaries.

Esso Chemical Company Inc

A 100% consolidated subsidiary of Standard Oil of New Jersey, it co-ordinates Esso's chemical business world-wide. In terms of sales, Esso's chemical activities rank second only to those of Shell companies among the world's major oil companies and cover a broadly similar range of products to Shell companies, including base chemicals, intermediates, plastics, elastomers and agricultural chemicals.

Farbenfabriken Bayer AG

West German company which produces dyestuffs, pharmaceuticals, plastics, synthetic rubber, pigments, inorganic chemicals, tanning agents, fibres and agricultural chemicals. With BASF and Hoechst, is one of the three biggest West German chemical companies. Has a controlling interest in Chemische Werke Huels and is an equal partner with BP in

Erdoelchemie in West Germany. It has large overseas interests with 400 production and sales subsidiaries in 19 countries, including a joint venture at Antwerp, Bayer-Shell Isocyanates NV.

Farbwerke Hoechst AG

West German chemical company, now the third largest in the world, with world-wide interests both through subsidiaries and associates, half of its sales being outside West Germany. Among its principal products are plastics, fibres, films, dyestuffs, cosmetics, pharmaceuticals and inorganic chemicals. It is a partner with a Shell company, amongst others, in Industrias Químicas Asociadas, which operates chemical plants at Tarragona in Spain.

Fina

Brand name appearing in names of subsidiaries of Petrofina SA.

General Sekiyu KK (General Oil Co)

Japanese company engaged in petroleum importing and marketing. Has interest in two refineries through an affiliate, General Sekiyu Seisei KK, which is owned jointly with Esso Standard Sekiyu KK. Other affiliates are General Gas KK – importer and marketer of liquefied petroleum gas, and General Kaiun KK (General Shipping Co Ltd), transporter of crude and LPG.

Getty Oil Company

The merger of Mission Development Company and its subsidiary Tidewater Oil Company became effective in September 1967, expanding Getty into an integrated international oil company. Getty holds an approximate 54·7% indirect interest in Skelly Oil Company, which continues as a separate enterprise, and a small interest in Iranian Oil Participants (IOP). Produces in Canada, the USA, the Kuwait/Saudi Arabia Neutral Zone and Algeria; refines in the Kuwait/Saudi Arabia Neutral Zone, Italy, Iran (through its interest in IOP) and in Japan (through a 48·7% interest in Mitsubishi Oil Company); markets Veedol lubricants in most countries and main products in some European countries and the Philippines. Has a petrochemical plant in operation near its Delaware refinery.

Golden Eagle
See Ultramar Company.

W R Grace
A major industrial US company, also operating in 45 overseas countries, which entered the chemical field in the early 1950s. Its chemical operations now account for over two-thirds of consolidated sales. Its wide product range includes agricultural and industrial chemicals, speciality chemicals, plastics and packaging materials, various consumer products including food processing agents and paper as well as interests in mining, transportation, petroleum refining and nuclear energy. In mid-1970 sold a number of Latin American holdings to Occidental.

Gulf Oil Corporation
US-based company which is engaged in all branches of the petroleum industry, controlling directly, or through its subsidiaries extensive production, pipeline, refining, petrochemicals, marine and marketing facilities.

Has a 50 % share in the Kuwait Oil Company; it also has a 7 % holding in Iranian Oil Participants; has refineries under construction near Milan and at Okinawa.

Home Oil Company Ltd
Canadian exploration, production, and transportation company holding oil and gas licences in the UK; has had natural gas strikes in Yorkshire. In 1968 Home Oil acquired all the outstanding shares of the Union Petroleum Corporation, a company engaged in the wholesale marketing of natural gas liquid products in the USA. Home Oil Co of Canada has acquired substantial land holdings in the North Slope area of Alaska.

Humble Oil and Refining Company
A wholly owned subsidiary of Standard Oil Company (New Jersey); engages in oil and gas exploration and production, refining, transportation and marketing in the USA. In 1968, a joint venture composed of Humble and Atlantic Richfield discovered significant reserves of oil and gas on the North Slope of Alaska. Humble is participating in a plan to construct a 48-inch pipeline across Alaska.

Idemitsu Kosan Company
A Japanese company engaged in oil refining, importing, exporting and marketing of petroleum products.

Imperial Chemical Industries (ICI)
A British company, the largest chemical manufacturer outside the USA and the second largest in the world. Has widely diversified chemical interests principally in basic organic chemicals and intermediates, inorganic chemicals, plastics, fibres, paints, dyestuffs and explosives. Also has interests in textiles, non-ferrous metals, oil refining and exploration. Recently announced plans to produce protein from natural gas. Overseas interests embrace subsidiary or associated companies in 45 countries. Acquired Atlas Chemical Industries in USA in 1971. Of the total ICI group sales overseas (which exceed those in the UK) over one half are manufactured by subsidiaries abroad. Its interests in refining and exploration include an oil refinery on Teesside jointly owned with Phillips Petroleum and membership of a consortium with Burmah Oil, which is drilling in the North Sea.

Imperial Oil Ltd
Standard Oil Company (NJ) holds a 70% (approx) interest. Engages in the exploration of minerals and in the production, refining, transportation and marketing of petroleum and chemical products in Canada. Imperial holds 30% interest in Syncrude Canada Ltd, formed to carry out research on tar sands recovery in the Athabasca region of Alberta. In 1969 Alberta government approval was received to construct an 80 000 b/d plant to recover oil from the tar sands.

International Egyptian Oil Company Inc
A subsidiary of ENI with interests in production in Egypt, through a 50% share in Compagnie Orientale des Pétroles d'Egypte (COPE).

Interprovincial Pipe Line Company
A Canadian company engaged in the transportation of crude petroleum by pipeline systems, mainly in Canada, but with a US section which is owned and operated by a wholly owned subsidiary, Lakehead Pipe Line Company.

Iraanse Aardolie Exploratie en Productie Maatschappij (Iranian Oil Exploration and Producing Company) NV
Iraanse Aardolie Raffinage Maatschappij (Iranian Oil Refining Company) NV
See Iranian Oil Participants (IOP).

Iran Pan American Oil Company (IPAC)
Owned equally by National Iranian Oil Company and Amoco Iran Oil Company. Produces offshore Iran.

Iranian Oil Participants (IOP)
Holding company formed in 1954 and owned by the following companies:

British Petroleum Company	40%
Netherlands Iranian Oil Trading Company (Royal Dutch/Shell)	14%
Iran California Oil Company (Standard Oil California)	7%
Esso Trading Company of Iran (Standard Oil Company (New Jersey))	7%
Mobil Oil Iran (Mobil Oil Corporation)	7%
Gulf International Company (Gulf Oil Corporation)	7%
Texaco Iran Limited (Texaco Incorporated)	7%
Compagnie Française des Pétroles (CFP)	6%
Iricon Agency (*see* Iricon Agency Limited)	5%

The participating companies formed two subsidiary companies: Iraanse Aardolie Exploratie en Productie Maatschappij (Iranian Oil Exploration and Producing Company) NV and Iraanse Aardolie Raffinage Maatschappij (Iranian Oil Refining Company) NV, known collectively as Iranian Oil Operating Companies, which are responsible for exploration and production in a defined area of south-western Iran, and for the operation of the refinery at Abadan. They exercise their rights on behalf of the National Iranian Oil Company.

Iranian Oil Services Limited (IROS)
Owned by the same companies as Iranian Oil Participants, it provides the Iranian Oil Operating Companies with services, etc outside Iran.

C

Iraq Petroleum Company Limited (IPC)
Owned 23·75% each by The Shell Petroleum Company Ltd, CFP, BP and Near-East Development Corporation, and 5% by Participations and Explorations Corporation; it has a concession in north-eastern Iraq, where it has production and pipelines to the Mediterranean. It has no sales organization. Laws enacted by the Iraq Government in 1961 and 1967 restricted IPC's rights and exploration activities.

Iricon Agency Ltd
Formed in 1955 to act as agents for the following US companies, which between them hold a 5% interest in IOP:

Iran Atlantic Company (Atlantic Richfield Company)	1/3 of 5%
American Independent Oil Company of Iran (American Independent Oil Company)	1/6 of 5%
Charter (Iran) Petroleum Company (Charter Oil Companies)	1/6 of 5%
Getty Iran Ltd (Getty Oil Company)	1/6 of 5%
San Jacinto Eastern Corporation (Continental Oil Company)	1/12 of 5%
Sohio-Iran Trading (Standard Oil Company (Ohio))	1/12 of 5%

Koa Oil Company
Caltex Petroleum Corporation holds a 50% interest in this Japanese refining company. The products are sold to Caltex Oil (Japan) and marketed through Nippon Oil Company. Operates refineries at Iwakuni and Osaka, Japan, daily capacity 229 000 barrels.

Kuwait National Petroleum Company (KNPC)
The Kuwait Government has a 60% holding in this company, which has sole rights for the distribution and sale of petroleum products in Kuwait. KNPC owns Kuwait's first national refinery, at Shuaiba, which came on stream during the third quarter of 1968, and has completed its first products terminal in Europe, at Copenhagen, the redistribution point for marketing the refinery's products, mainly in northern Europe. The company has a 5% participation in Central African Petroleum

Refineries (Pvt), and holds a 51% interest in an exploration and production venture with Hispanoil in Kuwait.

Kuwait Oil Company (KOC)

Owned jointly through subsidiaries by BP and Gulf; it is the company operating the Kuwait concession (on the mainland). Its functions are production, refining, storage and loading of crude and products on behalf of BP (Kuwait) Ltd and Gulf Kuwait Company.

Lago Oil and Transport Company

A wholly owned subsidiary of Standard Oil Company (New Jersey). The company, oil refiners and marketers, owns and operates a 440 000 b/d refinery at Aruba, Netherlands Antilles.

Lavan Petroleum Company (Lapco)

Owned 50% by National Iranian Oil Company (NIOC) and 12·5% each by Arco Exploration Company, Murphy Middle East Oil Company, Iranian Sun Oil Company and Union Oil Company of Iran; engaged in exploration, development and production. A pipeline has been completed from the Sassan offshore oilfield to the loading terminal on Lavan Island.

Libyan American Oil Company

A subsidiary of Atlantic Richfield, with a 25·5% interest in oil production from the Raguba field in Libya, and a 51% interest in two other concessions where exploratory drilling is in progress.

Marathon Oil Company

US company with production in Libya through an interest in the Oasis group, and with an interest of about 50% in extensive acreage in the Cook Inlet-Kenai Peninsula area of Alaska, where production commenced in 1967. Holds a 100% interest in an exploration agreement covering the entire Republic of Ireland and is also exploring in Colombia, the UK and Dutch sectors of the North Sea, Argentina and Papua. Refines and markets in Europe.

Maruzen Oil Company

Japanese independent company which is engaged in oil refining and the marketing of petroleum products and petrochemicals. The company owns four refineries and is one of three Japanese companies holding jointly a concession in offshore Abu Dhabi.

Mene Grande Oil Company (Meneg)

Wholly owned subsidiary of Transocean Gulf Oil Company, a subsidiary of the Gulf Oil Corporation. Holds producing and non-producing properties in Venezuela. Also owns a two-thirds interest in Venezuela Gulf Refining Company (Vengref).

Mitsubishi Oil Company

Japanese company in which Getty Oil Company holds just under 50% interest. It is a member of the Mitsubishi Industrial group. Its principal business lines are refining, importation and marketing of petroleum and petrochemicals. Has refineries at Kawasaki and Mizushima. Mitsubishi holds a 40% capital interest in Tohoku Oil Co which was formed in early 1969 to construct a refinery on Honshu Island.

Mobil Oil Corporation

US-based company, with just under half its sales and net income in the USA, which operates through affiliates in all branches of the petroleum industry internationally. It has a small crude-producing subsidiary in Venezuela, a 50% interest in Colombian Petroleum Company and production interests in the Eastern Hemisphere through a 10% holding in Aramco, an approximate 12% holding in the IPC companies, a 7% holding in IOP, and a subsidiary in Libya. Mobil has marketing activities throughout Europe, and since the break-up of Stanvac (except in Indonesia) has operated independently from Esso in East and South Africa, Asia and Australia. Also has chemical interests in USA and overseas.

Monsanto Company

A US company, whose principal products are synthetic fibres, plastics, resins and coatings, plasticizers, phosphates, detergents and agricultural products. Monsanto is the third largest chemical company in the USA where it has 43 plants and 13 research and development laboratories. Monsanto has manufacturing and marketing operations in more than 30 countries outside the USA, where sales amount to one-fifth of the company's total.

Montecatini-Edison SpA
Formed by the merger in 1966 of two large Italian companies, Montecatini, with chemical, mineral and metallurgical interests, and Edison, a chemical and electrical power producer. ENI and IRI have important shareholdings. Montedison produces a wide range of organic and inorganic chemicals, plastics, fibres, fertilizers and many other end-products. It has numerous subsidiaries and associates in Europe and North and South America, and is a partner with a Shell company in Rotterdamse Polyolefinen Mij, NV.

Mosul Petroleum Company
Owned by the same companies as Iraq Petroleum Company. Has a concession, from which it is producing, in the Mosul area of north-western Iraq.

Murphy Oil Corporation
US company with production in Venezuela, Canada and offshore Iran, through a 12·5% interest in Lavan Petroleum Company. Exploring in the UK sector of the North Sea as a member of the Burmah group and offshore Norway. Has a 16% interest in two Libyan concessions, and a 20% interest in an exploration venture in Yorkshire.

National Iranian Oil Company (NIOC)
Owned by the Iranian Government. Operates refineries and has others under construction. Has a 50% interest in SIRIP (with ENI) and Iran Pan American Oil Company (with Standard Indiana) producing in offshore Iran from the Darius field. NIOC and Pan American each have a 13% interest in a refinery and ammonia plant in Madras which came on stream in 1969 and which will be supplied with Darius crude. NIOC also has a 17·5% holding in a refinery in South Africa which went onstream early 1971 and, with CFP, will supply the refinery's crude oil needs. In October 1969 a

wholly owned subsidiary, Iran International Oil Corporation, was formed in the USA to market NIOC's Iranian crude.

Besides oil marketing and distribution, NIOC is also responsible for the operation and development of the country's petrochemical industries.

Near East Development Corporation (NEDCO)
Owned 50% by Standard Oil Company (New Jersey) and 50% by Mobil Oil Corporation. It has a 23·75% interest in IPC group of companies.

Nippon Oil Company
A Japanese company engaged in refining and marketing activities. Nippon Oil and Caltex each hold a 50% interest in Nippon Petroleum Refining Company, the products of which are supplied to Nippon Oil through Caltex.

Oasis Oil Company of Libya
Explores and produces in Libya on behalf of Marathon Oil Company, Continental Oil Company and Amerada Petroleum Corporation. There is a 50% Shell interest in the Amerada share.

Occidental Petroleum Corporation
US independent company with interests in the exploration and production of oil and natural gas in North America and extensive interests in fertilizer manufacture and marketing in USA and Canada. The company has undertaken several joint fertilizer ventures with governments in Morocco, Tunisia, Libya and Saudi Arabia, and has a one-third interest in plans to exploit sulphur in Saudi Arabia, through its subsidiary Jefferson Lake Sulphur Company. Has made large oil discoveries in its concessions in Libya, and crude oil deliveries, for European markets, commenced in February 1968. In February 1968 Occidental exercised its option to purchase Signal Oil and Gas Company's European refining and marketing operations. In January 1968, Occidental bought Island Creek Coal Company, the third largest US coal producer, and in July 1968 the company acquired Hooker Chemical Corporation, which will operate under its own name as a wholly owned subsidiary. Occidental chemical interests are the third largest among the oil companies. It is planned to construct an 80 000 b/d refinery on Canvey Island, UK.

Overseas Tankship Corporation
Owned by Caltex Petroleum Corporation and is responsible for the marine transportation of the Caltex group of companies.

Pacific Petroleums Ltd
Phillips Petroleum Company holds a 49% interest in the issued stock of this Canadian company. Engaged in exploration, producing, refining and marketing of crude oil and natural gas in Canada. Also participates with a group of major oil companies in developing concessions in Venezuela.

Pakistan Petroleum Ltd
Owned 70% by Burmah Oil Company, has discovered a number of gasfields in Pakistan and Bangladesh and produces from three of them. Crude oil is produced from Balkassar oilfield and is refined in association with Attock Oil Company.

Participations and Explorations Corporation (Partex)
Owns a 5% interest in Iraq Petroleum Company Ltd and also holds an interest in Basrah Petroleum Company Ltd, Mosul Petroleum Company Ltd, Qatar Petroleum Company Ltd, Petroleum Development (Cyprus), Abu Dhabi Petroleum Company Ltd, Petroleum Services (Middle East) Ltd, Syria Petroleum Company Ltd and Petroleum Development (Oman) Ltd.

Petrofina SA
A Belgian independent which is exploring actively in many countries and now has production in the USA, Canada and Angola, as well as refining, tanker and marketing interests mainly in Europe; its activities cover many countries in Europe and North and West Africa. It has interests in concessions in the UK and Norwegian sectors of the North Sea and a developing petrochemical business in the hands of its affiliate Petrochim.

Petróleo Brasileiro SA (Petrobrás)
80·1% Government-owned company supervising all branches of the petroleum industry in Brazil. Has production and began

exploration work offshore during 1968. Owns and operates refineries and also has a tanker fleet. Petrobrás Química SA, in which Petróleo Brasileiro SA will hold not less than 51% interest, was formed in 1968 to develop the petrochemical industry. The Petrobrás fertilizer plant and synthetic rubber plant have been transferred to the new company. The Government through Petrobrás is concentrating its resources on intensifying its refining activities, its large rubber plant, tanker fleet and pipelines. Petrobrás has budgeted $1 billion to be spent for enlarging and improving its facilities.

Petróleos Mexicanos (Pemex)
The Mexican state petroleum company, with complete control of the country's oil industry. Actively engaged in exploration, production from oil and gas fields both onshore and offshore, refining and marketing, and chemical manufacture.

Pétroles de l'Atlantique (ANTAR)
A French company engaged in refining and marketing. Operates refineries at Donges, Vern-sur-Seiche and in the Valenciennes area. Holds 4% participation in Soc du Pipe-Line Sud-Européen and 31·66% in Raffinerie de Strasbourg SA.

Petromin
Saudi Arabian Governmental agency, formed to engage in all phases of the oil and mineral industries, industrial developments, etc. A 15 000 b/d refinery is being constructed near Riyadh, scheduled to start operation in 1972.

Phillips Petroleum Company
An integrated US company with production in Venezuela and Canada; a 50% share in ENI's Nigerian discovery and a 50% share in a major Egyptian find. Is exploring in many countries, including offshore Iran and Australia, the North Sea and in Alaska, where it has a 25% interest in acreage in the Cook Inlet area. A plant operated by Phillips Petroleum has been built on Alaska's Kenai Peninsula to liquefy gas for transportation to Japan in refrigerated tankers. Phillips has an interest in refineries in India and the UK (with ICI), and has oil and gas properties in Canada through a 49% interest in Pacific Petroleums. Company engages in every phase of the

petroleum industry and many related petrochemical and chemical activities, e.g. synthetic rubber, plastics, chemical fertilizers, carbon black, raw materials for synthetic fibres, films, resins, etc.

Qatar Petroleum Company (QPC)
Owned by the same parent companies and in the same proportion as Iraq Petroleum Company; produces from a concession in Qatar.

Rhône-Poulenc
Rhône-Poulenc, already the largest chemical company in France, increased its interest in chemical manufacture when in 1969 it acquired Progil and a majority holding in Péchiney/St Gobain. In turn this company has now merged with Progil to form Rhône–Progil. Textiles which had until then accounted for more than half of Rhône-Poulenc's total production now account for only about one-third. Has some seventy plants and laboratories throughout France while major subsidiaries are located in the UK, Switzerland, West Germany, Spain, Italy, Brazil, Argentina and the USA.

Signal Companies Inc
Formerly Signal Oil and Gas Company. An integrated US company with production in Argentina and Iran (through interest in Charter Company) and exploration permits in the Caribbean, Canada, Spain and Ghana. The company is also a participant in North Sea exploration, holding a 10% interest in Dutch acreage. Occidental Petroleum will earn a 50% interest in Signal's holdings offshore and onshore Jamaica and Honduras according to an agreement signed in late 1969. In a contract signed in August 1967, Signal agreed to act as exclusive agent for the sale of all Occidental Petroleum Corporation's Libyan crude oil for a ten-year period. In February 1968 Signal sold its refining and marketing interests in Europe to Occidental Petroleum.

Skelly Oil Company
US company in which Getty Oil Company has a controlling interest; engaged in all branches of the petroleum industry in

the USA. Is a member of a group drilling offshore Iran and was granted an exploration concession in Mozambique late in 1967. The company also holds a 25% interest in acreage in the Cook Inlet area of Alaska. Wholly owned Skelly Oil of Canada was formed in 1970 to conduct exploration and production in Canada.

Sociedade Anónima Concessionaria da Refinação de Petróleos em Portugal (SACOR)
The Portuguese Government has a one-third interest in SACOR, which operates two refineries. The company is guaranteed a market for its products to the extent of 50% of the consumption of continental Portugal.

Società Azionaria Raffinazione Olii Minerali (SAROM)
Owns and operates a refinery in Italy; also has a majority share interest in Pibigas, marketers of LPG.

Società per Azioni Raffineria Padana Olii Minerali (SARPOM)
Owned 64% (approx) by Esso Italiana, 26% by Chevron Oil Europe and 10% by Texaco Operations (Europe). Owns and operates a refinery in Italy which is linked by pipeline to the tanker terminal near Savona.

Société Nationale des Pétroles d'Aquitaine (SNPA) (Aquitaine)
Owned 51% by ERAP, SNPA operates mainly in France but also participates in exploration and production throughout the world through its subsidiaries and interests in various companies. Aquitaine participates in groups exploring in the UK, Dutch and Norwegian sectors of the North Sea. (*See* Total).

Société Nationale de Recherches et d'Exploitation des Pétroles en Algérie (SN Repal)
A company owned 50% by the Algerian Government and 50% by the French Government and various French finance companies. Jointly with CFP (Algérie), the company produces crude from the Hassi Messaoud fields in Algeria, and also operates a small refinery there.

Société Nationale pour la Recherche, la Production, le Transport, la Transformation, et la Commercialisation des Hydrocarbures (Sonatrach)

Algerian state-owned company participating in all phases of the oil industry. Sonatrach operates a fleet of tankers and also directly controls areas ceded to it by the Algerian Government in which exploration and development is in progress. In January 1967 Sonatrach took over BP's distribution network in Algeria and by June 1968 it had completed its nationalization of all the foreign-owned marketing properties in the country. Sonatrach has commenced selling crude oil in its own right, becoming interested in the European and South American markets, and is also interested in selling natural gas internationally. In January 1970, Sonatrach acquired all of Sinclair Petroleum's assets in Algeria which had been expropriated by the Algerian Government in 1969. A refinery is being constructed at Skikda and is expected on stream in 1972.

South African Coal, Oil and Gas Corporation (Sasol)

All the shares are held by a Government-sponsored company. Manufactures liquid fuel and chemicals from coal, markets through a subsidiary and has a 50% interest in a company exploring for oil and gas onshore and offshore South Africa. Sasol holds a 52·5% interest in a refinery which went on stream early in 1971 near Sasolburg, CFP having a 30% interest and NIOC a 17·5% holding.

Standard Oil Company of California (Socal)

An integrated US company, deriving approximately half its net income from the USA. Its main Eastern Hemisphere interests are its 30% holding in Aramco, its 7% holding in Iranian Oil Participants, its 50% interest in Amoseas and its 50% share in Caltex. Since the split in the assets and operations of Caltex in Europe, the co-ordination and management of Socal's share of these operations is being carried out by Chevron Oil Europe. In October 1968 a new subsidiary – Chevron Overseas Petroleum – was formed to direct its foreign exploration and production activities, and in Belgium a 130 000 b/d refinery is being constructed. Has quite substantial chemical interests.

Standard Oil Company (Indiana) (Amoco)

US independent with many overseas exploration ventures. Through subsidiaries it has interest in production in Venezuela, Argentina, Libya and Egypt and in Iran through its 50% share in Iran Pan American Oil Company (jointly owned with NIOC). It is actively developing its outlets outside North America and has refining and marketing interests in Australia and Europe and a 13% interest in the Madras refinery in India which came on stream at the beginning of 1969. Amoco is the operator for the British Gas Council-Amoco group, exploring and producing in the North Sea. Has substantial chemical interests.

Standard Oil Company (New Jersey) (Esso)

The largest of the majors in terms of sales, assets and income. It is US based and earns approximately half of its net income inside the USA. Has important interests elsewhere in the Western Hemisphere, 70% (approx) of Imperial Oil and just over 95% of Creole, the largest companies in Canada and Venezuela respectively. In the Eastern Hemisphere, Esso has crude production through its 30% share in Aramco, its 12% share in the IPC group of companies, its 7% holding in Iranian Oil Participants and its Libyan interests. It operates through subsidiaries in Europe. Until March 1962 it marketed in East and South Africa, Asia and Australia through its 50% interest (with Mobil) in Stanvac. Since the break-up of Stanvac, Esso has operated independently in these areas, except in Indonesia. In 1969 the company concluded arrangements for construction of a 72 000 b/d refinery in Okinawa, due for completion in early 1972. (*See* Esso Chemical Company Inc).

Standard Oil Company (Ohio) (Sohio)

US company with production, through its shareholding in IOP, in Iran. On 1 January 1970 Standard Oil Co acquired all the outstanding capital stock of BP (Holdings) Inc, of which BP Oil Corporation is the major subsidiary in exchange for 1000 shares of Sohio Special stock equivalent to a 25% common stock interest in Sohio, which interest will increase as sustainable net crude oil production from the Prudhoe Bay, Alaska, properties rises above 200 000 b/d, and will reach a maximum of approximately 54% if such production reaches 600 000 b/d prior to 1 January 1978. As a result of the Sohio-BP merger, the company acquired various working interests in mineral leases on the North Slope of Alaska.

PT Stanvac Indonesia
Joint Esso and Mobil company which explores and produces in Indonesia.

Sun Oil Company (Sunoco)
US independent with production in Venezuela and widespread exploration interests (North Sea, offshore Iran (*See* Lavan), Alaska, Saudi Arabia, Nigeria, Australia, Argentina, etc); markets speciality lubricants and is extending the range of its European marketing. Effective 25 October 1968, the company merged with Sunray DX Oil Co. Sunoco will own an 80% interest in a fertilizer complex being constructed on the islands of Martinique and Guadeloupe. The company owns seven tankers and also holds a 67% interest in Liberia Refining Company, which owns a 10 000 b/d refinery near Monrovia.

Tenneco Incorporated
Formerly Tennessee Gas Transmission, involved principally in the transportation of natural gas in the US. Through wholly owned subsidiaries, engages in oil production, refining and marketing, chemicals and packaging. Has oil and gas production in the USA, Canada and Venezuela, and oil concessions offshore the Malagasy Republic, Thailand, Argentina and in the Dutch North Sea. In 1966 Tenneco began marketing in the UK and early in 1968 acquired an interest in a Dutch marketing firm. In 1967, Tenneco acquired Kern County Land Company, which has oil interests in the USA, Canada and Australia.

Texaco Incorporated
US-based company, very strongly placed inside the US, where more than half its net income is earned. Has subsidiaries in Canada, Colombia, Venezuela and Trinidad engaged in exploration, production, refining and marketing activities. Its major crude producing interests are in the Middle East, where it has a 30% share in Aramco's Saudi Arabian production and a 7% holding in Iranian Oil Participants. Texaco is a joint parent (with Standard Oil Company of California) of Caltex,

which through its subsidiaries has operations in more than 60 countries. Through Caltex, Texaco markets in most of the Eastern Hemisphere but, since the split in the assets and operations of Caltex in Europe, has carried out these refining and marketing activities separately (*see* Texaco Ltd). A new refinery came on stream late in 1968 in Belgium. In West Germany, name of DEA changed to Deutsche Texaco AG in 1970.

Texaco Ltd
Regent Oil Company, a UK marketer, changed its name to Texaco Limited as a result of the division of the Caltex assets in Europe. Regent used to be a part of Caltex, although 75% owned by Texaco. It has now been taken over completely, except for 100 service stations which have been transferred to Standard Oil Company of California.

Total
Name under which Compagnie Française des Pétroles (CFP) markets. In December 1971 chemical interests were associated with those of Aquitaine and ELF/ERAP in new company, ATO.

Trans-Arabian Pipe Line Company (Tapline)
Has the same parents and shareholding as Aramco; operates the pipeline that runs from Saudi Arabia to the Mediterranean port of Sidon, Lebanon.

TransCanada Pipe Lines
Owns and operates a natural gas pipeline system extending from Alberta to Montreal. Exports natural gas into Minnesota and Wisconsin by means of a loopline and also has a loopline into Ontario, for export to northern New York State. Has a joint interest in Great Lakes Gas Transmission Company, which is operating a new pipeline from Manitoba to Ontario. The pipeline serves as a loop of the Trans-Canada transmission system. Also conducts oil and gas exploration in Canada through wholly owned subsidiaries.

Trans Mountain Oil Pipe Line Company
Owns and operates a crude oil pipeline system from Edmonton, Alberta, to near Vancouver, British Columbia, and serves a

number of refineries. A spur-line runs from the border in British Columbia into Washington, USA, and this section is owned and operated by a US subsidiary – Trans Mountain Oil Pipe Line Corporation.

Turkish Petroleum Corporation
(Turkiye Petrolleri Anonim Ortakligi) (TPAO)
Owned 51% by the Turkish Government, has exploration, production, pipeline and refining rights under the Petroleum Act of Turkey. Owns a number of producing fields, linked by pipelines to its refinery at Batman. A second refinery, near Izmir, is scheduled for completion by mid-1972. Also holds a 55% interest in Petrochemicals Corporation, which operates a petrochemicals plant in Yarimca (Izmit).

Ultramar Company
British independent company owning, through its subsidiary Caracas Petroleum SA (CPSA), 50% of Las Mercedes, which has producing interests in Venezuela. Has refining interests in Panama, and, through Golden Eagle subsidiaries, refining and marketing interests in the USA, Canada and the UK. Holds interests in North Sea acreage.

Union Carbide Corporation
The second largest chemical manufacturer in the USA, it also has extensive non-chemical interests including metals, industrial gases, electronic and nuclear products, food and packaging products. Operates on an international basis and has about 400 plants, laboratories and mines around the world. Recently formed a joint venture with Singer General Precision Inc, and Ocean Systems Inc, to develop advanced diving systems and new breathing gas mixtures for underwater activities.

Union Oil Company of California
US company. Has oil production from Alaska's Cook Inlet as well as production from the Kenai gasfield in Alaska, and oil production in Australia and Venezuela. Has exploration interests in many countries outside North America, notably in the Middle East (including offshore Iran through a 12·5% interest in Lavan Petroleum Company) and in Kalimantan, Italy, Nicaragua and Thailand.

Venezuela Gulf Refining Company (Vengref)
Owned two-thirds by Gulf (through Mene Grande Oil Company) and one-third by Texaco: operates a refinery in Venezuela.

VIP Petroleum
Importer and distributor of petroleum products in the UK. A subsidiary of Occidental Petroleum (was acquired from Signal Oil under its European option).

Wintershall AG
Owned over 95% by Badische Anilin-und Soda-Fabrik (BASF). Participates in exploration in the Norwegian and Dutch sectors of the North Sea, Libya, the Middle East and Eastern Peru. Also has exploration and production in Western Canada through its wholly owned subsidiary, Wintershall Oil of Canada, and owns a 15% interest in Aral. Owns 18·5% participation in DEMINEX, the West German exploration company and operates three refineries in West Germany.

Yacimientos Petrolíferos Fiscales (YPF)
The Argentine state oil corporation, which owns and operates oilfields, pipelines, refineries and tankers in Argentina.

Yacimientos Petrolíferos Fiscales Bolivianos (YPFB)
The Bolivian state oil company, which has exploration and production in Bolivia and owns and operates refineries which are connected by pipelines to Arica, the Chilean port on the Pacific coast.

Finance (World)

Capital employed

The oil industry* is one of the largest and most complex industries in the world. It is also very capital intensive. For United States companies for example in 1970, the amount of capital invested per employee was about four and a half times the average for all United States industry.

At the end of 1970, the original cost of the property, plant and equipment in use by the oil industry is estimated to have been $205 850 million. Approximately half of this figure represented investment in the United States and almost two-thirds of the total investment was owned by United States companies.

In 1971 oil production rose by approximately 5·8 % over the previous year to 15 300 million barrels for the year – or about 42 million barrels each day. This compares with an average annual growth rate of 7·8 % for the period 1960–1970.

To meet the existing demand for oil and to prepare for its expected growth, the oil industry in 1970 spent over $21 400 million, including $1300 million for exploration. This represents an increase of 8·6 % over the previous year. In the ten years from 1961 to 1970 the industry spent more than $156 500 million on capital and exploration projects, of which approximately one half was in the United States.

In 1971 the combined capital expenditure of the seven major international groups of oil companies amounted to $7903 million, 14 % more than in 1970. The financing of this expenditure is shown in the table on the next page. From these figures it is clear that retained earnings and depreciation provisions provided the major portion. This situation has been typical of the oil industry for a long time, although the proportion of debt financing is increasing. Long-term debt as a percentage of total capital employed for the seven major international groups of oil companies rose from 8·3 % in 1961 to 11·3 % in 1966 and to 19·0 % in 1971.

*Excludes the USSR, Eastern Europe and China in this chapter.

Nonetheless it appears inevitable that the industry will continue to find the bulk of its capital needs from its own sources because it would be impracticable to raise such large sums on the capital market each year. Consequently adequate profits must be made to finance expansion as well as to preserve the industry's financial standing so that it can, where appropriate, attract additional funds, on reasonable terms, from the capital markets.

| | 1971 | | 1967-1971 | |
	$ million	%	$ million	%
Capital expenditure	7903		33975	
Financed by:				
Retained earnings	2637	33	11151	33
Depreciation provisions	3986	50	17158	50
Net new long-term borrowing	1942	25	6789	20
Additional funds from				
shareholders	223	3	745	2
Other items net	(885)	(11)	(1868)	(5)
	7903	100	33975	100

Profitability

This begs the question as to what are 'adequate' profits. There is no indisputable way of measuring profitability, particularly in periods of rapid inflation, when the money unit in which results are expressed has declining purchasing power. Nonetheless one can get an idea of the trend of oil industry profitability and how this compares with that of other industries by looking at the rate of return on net assets. This is a widely used yardstick (sometimes also described as 'return on shareholders' investment', 'return on equity', 'return on net worth' or 'return on shareholders' funds') and represents the net income of a business for the period in question expressed as a percentage of the capital employed in the business, net of the amounts borrowed. Looking at it another way, the return can be described as net income as a percentage of the capital contributed by shareholders by subscribing for shares, and by ploughing back earnings instead of receiving them as dividends.

The world-wide rate of return on average net assets for a group of 28 petroleum companies covered in a survey published by the Chase Manhattan Bank, representing more than

75% of the original cost of the property, plant and equipment in use by the oil industry dropped from 11% in 1969 to 10·3% in 1970. In the United States the rate of return fell from 10·9% in 1969 to 9·9% in 1970. Outside the United States the decline was from 11·1% in 1969 to 11% in 1970. It was the first year since 1958 that the rate of return declined simultaneously both in the United States and in the rest of the world. For comparison, the average rate of return for manufacturing industry in the United States (according to *Fortune* magazine) was 9·5% in 1970, while outside the United States the comparable figure was 8·3%.

Eastern Hemisphere net earnings per barrel for 7 majors

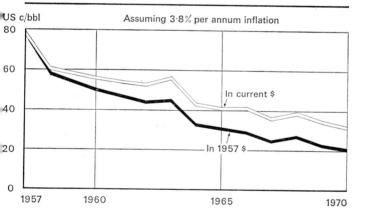

The First National City Bank of New York has for a number of years charted the progress of the Eastern Hemisphere operations of the seven major international groups of oil companies. The bank calculates that net income declined from around 78 cents per barrel in 1957 to under 33 cents per barrel in 1970. If we correct these figures for inflation the real returns are reduced to about 20 cents per barrel of 1957 money in 1970.

For the same group of companies, the rate of return on net assets declined from 18·6% in 1957 to 11·2% in 1970.

The main long term factors causing the decline in net income per barrel have been continuing competitive pressure on product selling prices, inflationary rises in costs together with increases in tax and royalty payments to governments.

Taxation

Tax and royalty payments in the Eastern Hemisphere are estimated‡ to have been around $1·25 per barrel in 1971 as compared with 71 cents per barrel in 1960, and 86 cents per barrel in 1970. Payments to governments rose steeply following the agreements of 1971 which provided for immediate increases in the posted prices of crude oil, and in most producing areas an increase in the rate of tax to 55%. Further increases to posted prices reflecting the changed value of the US dollar were made early in 1972, and continuing increases over the years to 1976 were provided for in the 1971 agreements.

Estimated government revenues from oil in some OPEC countries over the last few years are as follows:

	1965	1966	1967	1968	1969	1970
	\$ million					
Venezuela	1135	1112	1254	1253	1289	1406
Libya	371	476	631	952	1132	1295
Saudi Arabia†	655	777	852	966	1008	1200
Iran	522	593	737	817	938	1076
Kuwait†	671	707	718	766	812	896
Iraq	375	394	361	476	483	513

†Including half-share of Neutral Zone

The total income tax paid by the seven majors in 1971 amounted to $8694 million, 51% more than in 1970, although the increase of net income* was only 10%.

The major groups of oil companies

Despite the development of many independent and government-sponsored companies in recent years, the influence of the seven major groups of oil companies on the oil scene

‡ Final figures not available at the time of going to press.
* After deduction of extraordinary charges

remains considerable. In 1970 they supplied 56% of the world's oil demand, and accounted for 35% of total oil industry capital expenditures. To give an idea of the relationship that exists between the profits they earn and the enormous investment required to generate these profits, the following table gives some figures from their accounts for 1971.

In considering these figures it should be remembered that cost inflation over the years has raised the cost of equipment etc to such a degree that to replace today all the assets currently in use would require an expenditure significantly greater than their original cost as included in the figures for average net assets.

	Average net assets 1971	Net income* 1971	Return on average net assets 1971
	\$ million		%
Standard (New Jersey)	11272	1462	13·0
Royal Dutch/Shell	9861	847	9·2†
Texaco	6512	904	13·9
Gulf	5400	561	10·4
Mobil	4686	541	11·5
Standard California	4783	511	10·7
British Petroleum	3568	379	10·1†

In 1971 these companies paid out in total \$2746 million in dividends, 53% of net income (57% in 1970).

† Calculated on underlying £ figures
* After deduction of extraordinary charges

Finance (Shell)

Royal Dutch/Shell Group companies supplied approximately 15% of all the oil sold in the world† in 1971. Group companies in total continued to be the second largest enterprise in the world oil industry. Net assets employed totalled £3884 million.

	1970		1971	
			£ million	
Assets and liabilities				
Property, plant and equipment	6657		7306	
Less depreciation etc	3003		3247	
		3654		4059
Investments		400		458
Cash and securities		546		554
Working capital and other assets and liabilities (net)		389		297
Capital employed		4989		5368
Long-term debt		761		964
Minority interests		527		520
Net assets		3701		3884

† Excludes the USSR, Eastern Europe and China in this chapter

	1970	1971
		£ million

Income account

Sales proceeds* –oil and natural gas	3779		4327
–chemicals		546	581
–mining and metals		45	123
		4370	5031
Other revenues		146	192
Share of earnings of associated companies		55	70
Interest income		60	53
		4631	5346
Purchases and operating expenses etc		3175	3603
Exploration		112	126
Research		50	53
Depreciation etc		331	383
Interest expense		64	85
Taxation on income		465	666
Minority interests		43	38
		4240	4954
Net income before extraordinary charge		391	392
Non-recurring charge arising from realignment of currencies in 1971†		—	22
Net income for the year		391	370
Appropriation for additional depreciation		24	22
Balance of net income for the year		367	348
Dividends – Royal Dutch		112	112
Dividends – Shell Transport		75	75
Retained earnings		180	161

* Net of sales taxes of £2139 million in 1970 and £2277 million in 1971

† This charge arises from the effect of changes in exchange rates on the assets and liabilities of Group companies when expressed in sterling.

	1970	1971
		£ million

Source and disposition of funds

	1970	1971
Retained earnings (including minority)	*231	*181
Depreciation etc added back	331	383
Increase in long-term debt	101	203
Other items (net)	(61)	83
	602	850
deduct:		
Capital expenditure	670	784
Increase (decrease) in investments	—	58
Net increase (decrease) in cash holdings	(68)	8

Ratios

	1970	1971
Return on average net assets (after extraordinary charge in 1971)	10·2%	9·2%
Income before extraordinary charge (including minority) per imp gal of sales	0·46p	0·45p
Equity in balance of Group net income before extraordinary charge		
Royal Dutch (60%):		
N fl per N fl 20 ordinary share	14·26	14·15
US $ equivalent†	3·94	4·04
Shell Transport (40%):		
new pence per 25p (5s 0d) ordinary share	28·29	28·41
US $ equivalent per New York share†	2·72	2·77

Capital expenditure was £784 million, £114 million higher than in 1970. Research and exploration expenses amounted to £179 million.

* Includes appropriation for additional depreciation
† Exchange rates used: 1971 £1 = $2.43   3.51 N. fl. = $1
                        1970 £1 = $2.40   3.62 N. fl. = $1

Profits in perspective

The Royal Dutch/Shell Group of companies as a whole earned 9·2% return on the average net assets invested in its world-wide operations.

The balance of net income (including minority interests but before the extraordinary charge) represented 5·4% of gross revenues. Of this amount the shareholders received about 3·0% and the remaining 2·4% together with the funds set aside to cover depreciation, was reinvested in the business for the replacement of existing property, plant and equipment and to provide for expansion.

Each £1 gross revenue was accounted for as follows:

Operating costs		0·51
Sales taxes and income taxes		0·39
Reinvestment for replacement and expansion		
Depreciation	0·05	
Net income retained		
(including minority interests)	0·02	
		0·07
Dividends to shareholders		
(including minority interests)		0·03
		1·00

Over the last ten years Group companies have more than doubled their sales volumes and in order to do so have had to find additional capital of £5600 million. Of these capital needs, 85% was met by reinvesting retained earnings and depreciation funds in the business: the remaining 15% was obtained from outside the business. The approximate split of Group net assets and Group net income in 1971 between the major areas of the world was as follows:

	Group net assets	Group net income
United States	19%	22%
Rest of Western Hemisphere	15%	24%
Europe and rest of Eastern Hemisphere	66%	54%

Parent companies' share capital

NV Koninklijke Nederlandsche Petroleum Maatschappij (Royal Dutch Petroleum Company) is incorporated in the Netherlands; fully paid capital is N fl 2 680 370 440 in ordinary shares of N fl 20 each and N fl 1 500 000 in preference shares.

The "Shell" Transport and Trading Company, Limited is incorporated in the United Kingdom: issued and fully paid capital comprises £138 104 302 in ordinary shares of 25p each and £12 000 000 in preference shares.

The shares in these companies are directly held by about a million shareholders living in many parts of the world (not allowing for indirect holdings through mutual funds, unit trusts, pension funds etc); the following figures show broadly where they are:

	Royal Dutch	"Shell" Transport	Combined
		% of total	
United Kingdom	4	95	41
Netherlands	34	—	20
United States	24	1	15
Switzerland	19	—	11
France	14	3	10
Others	5	1	3

Shares of the two parent companies are quoted on the leading stock exchanges in Europe, and also in New York. Unless local regulations prevent dealings in shares of foreign companies, the shares can be freely bought and sold by anyone anywhere, through stockbrokers and banks, at the price set by market supply and demand.

Future outlook

Prediction is particularly difficult against the background of the changes which marked 1971 and are still continuing. A flexible energy supply is essential to the functioning of our modern society and the contribution of oil to this vital supply will increase, since alternative energy sources such as nuclear power cannot yet make a significant contribution. There is considerable uncertainty particularly as to the future actions of governments *vis-à-vis* the oil companies, and the progress of inflation with its attendant problems. Nonetheless basic supply and demand considerations indicate that the oil industry should prosper, and Group companies are well placed to share in this prosperity.

Further details of the finances of Group companies can be obtained from the Annual Reports of the Royal Dutch Petroleum Company, and The "Shell" Transport and Trading Company, Limited. In addition, a detailed booklet is prepared each year giving financial and operational information for the Royal Dutch/Shell Group of companies for the preceding ten-year period. This booklet is published both in sterling and in US dollar equivalents. Here are some extracts:

Group financial statistics 1967-71

	1967	1968	1969	1970	1971
					£ million
Gross income	4488	5663	6112	6770	7623
Sales taxes etc	1389	1724	1932	2139	2277
Operational costs	2254	2827	2986	3337	3782
Depreciation etc	257	279	294	331	383
Taxation on income	248	340	376	465	666
Balance of net income	266	360	394	367	348
Capital expenditure	464	553	593	670	784
Cash and short-term securities	541	657	614	546	554
Net working capital	863	1006	1024	992	931
Long-term debt	568	603	660	761	964
Net assets	3019	3255	3497	3701	3884
Balance of net income after extraordinary charge as % of average net assets	9·0	11·5	11·7	10·2	9·2
Balance of net income before extraordinary charge (including minority) as % of gross income	6·7	7·4	7·3	6·1	5·4
Balance of net income before extraordinary charge (including minority) in pence per imp gal of sales	0·46p	0·57p	0·56p	0·46p	0·45p

Exploration and production (World)

Exploration

Exploration activity in 1971 continued at a high level, with increasing attention given to the exploration of marine areas off the coasts of all five continents.

Offshore exploration successes occurred in the UK, Norwegian, Danish and Netherlands parts of the North Sea, and in African, Middle Eastern, Indonesian and Australian waters.

On land new oil and gas strikes were reported in many countries (e.g. Canadian Arctic, Ecuador, Peru, the Netherlands, the USSR, Libya, Nigeria, Saudi Arabia, Indonesia and Australia).

Production

Total world production of crude oil and natural gas liquids (i.e. liquids extracted from natural gas) averaged 50·0 million b/d during 1971, compared with some 47·5 million b/d during 1970, an increase of 5·3 %.

In the Western Hemisphere production remained at about the same level. Only Canada achieved a marked percentage increase (+ 8·3%). This was offset by lower production in Venezuela (— 4·0%). Total output of the Western Hemisphere in 1971 was 35·9% of total world production.

Production in Africa decreased by 6·4%. The bulk of the decrease was in Algeria (—29·6%), following nationalisation measures and Libya (—17·2%), mainly due to the application of rules imposing limits on individual well and field production rates.

Production in Nigeria averaged 1 532 000 b/d during 1971, compared with 1 084 000 b/d during 1970 (+41·3%).

In the Middle East countries production expanded 17·4%, a growth of over 2·4 million b/d, with the main increases coming from Saudi Arabia (+26·8%), Iran (+18·7%) and Abu Dhabi (+35·3%). Output from the Middle East in 1971 contributed 32·6% of total world production, 3·4% more than in 1970.

The Far East/Australasia increase was 16·0 %, mainly from Australia (+70·4 %), and Malaysia (+282·3 %). Even so total production from this area averaged only 1 652 000 b/d during 1971.

Costs of exploration and production

Exploration calls for tremendous expenditures and the risk of failure is high. A seismic survey party on land may cost more than £60 000 a month and a similar party offshore may cost up to £200 000 a month.

A land exploration well may cost more than £250 000 to drill; offshore drilling and development may cost three to four times more than a similar operation on land.

Developing a new field is even more costly than exploration. A major oilfield can represent an investment of £300 million and it may take many years to reach pay-off.

World production of crude oil and natural gas liquids*

(daily average in thousands of barrels)

	1970	1971
North America		
USA	11 312	11 230
Canada	1 477	1 600
	12 789	12 830
Rest of Western Hemisphere		
Venezuela	3 715	3 565
Mexico	487	483
Argentina	392	425
Colombia	226	222
Brazil	166	170
Trinidad	140	130
Peru	75	65
Chile	39	42

	1970	1971
Bolivia	24	37
Ecuador	4	4
Cuba	2	2
	5 270	5 145
Europe		
West Germany	147	147
Yugoslavia	57	60
France	62	54
Austria	54	48
Netherlands	37	33
Italy	27	24
Norway	0	6
Spain	3	3
UK	2	3
	389	378

* Produced from natural gas by means of an extraction process

	1970	1971
Africa		
Libya	3 314	2 744
Nigeria	1 084	1 532
Algeria	1 022	720
Egypt	393	410
Gabon	109	114
Angola, Cabinda	98	113
Tunisia	88	87
Morocco	1	1
Congo (Brazzaville)	negl	negl
	6 109	5 721
Middle East		
Iran	3 845	4 565
Saudi Arabia	3 549	4 501
Kuwait	2 735	2 925
Iraq	1 565	1 711
Abu Dhabi	694	939
Neutral Zone	500	551
Qatar	362	430
Oman	332	294
Dubai	84	125
Syria	81	125

	1970	1971
Bahrein	77	75
Turkey	69	68
Israel	2	2
	13 895	16 311
Far East and Australasia		
Indonesia	854	904
Australia	179	305
India	140	145
Brunei	139	131
Malaysia	18	69
Afghanistan	47	50
Burma	18	19
Japan	16	15
Bangladesh	10	9
New Zealand	1	2
Others	2	3
	1 424	1 652
USSR, Eastern Europe and China	7 652	8 000
World total	47 528	50 037

Change in production of crude oil and natural gas liquids

	1971	Change from 1970
	thousands b/d	%
USA	— 82	— 0·7
Canada	+ 123	+ 8·3
Rest of Western Hemisphere	— 125	— 2·4
Europe	— 11	— 2·8
Africa	— 388	— 6·4
Middle East	+2416	+17·4
Far East/Australasia	+ 228	+16·0
USSR, Eastern Europe, China	+ 348	+ 4·5
World total	+2509	+ 5.3

Percentage of total by areas – 1971

USA	22·4	Middle East	32·6
Canada	3·2	Far East/	
Rest of Western		Australasia	3·3
Hemisphere	10·3	USSR, Eastern	
Europe	0·8	Europe, China	16·0
Africa	11·4		

World proven reserves of crude oil

Proven reserves are the quantities of oil and gas known to be present in formations that have been drilled, and commercially recoverable by present-day techniques at current costs and price levels.

Reserves from supplementary methods, such as the injection of water, gas and steam, are included. Research is being carried out to increase recovery efficiency, and advances in recovery techniques will continue to make an important contribution to reserves.

Over three-fifths of the world's present proven oil reserves lie in the Middle East; the presently proven reserves in Europe account for 1 % of the world's total proven reserves. The percentages by area are as follows:

North America	9	Far East/Australasia	2
Rest of Western		USSR, Eastern Europe,	
Hemisphere	5	and China	12
Middle East	62	Europe	1
		Africa	9

Details are as follows:

	millions of barrels		millions of barrels
North America		Colombia	1 580
USA	39 001	Argentina	1 573
Canada	8 559	Brazil	857
	47 560	Trinidad	605
		Peru	500
Rest of Western		Bolivia	300
Hemisphere		Chile	120
Venezuela	14 041	Cuba	1
Ecuador	6 000		28 777
Mexico	3 200		

	millions of barrels
Europe	
Norway	3 500
UK	1 000
West Germany	545
Denmark	500
Yugoslavia	315
Italy	305
Netherlands	230
Austria	190
France	120
Spain	100
	6 805
Africa	
Libya	30 000
Algeria	8 098
Nigeria	5 600
Egypt	3 000
Angola/Cabinda	750
Gabon	485
Tunisia	380
Morocco	9
Congo (Brazzaville)	5
	48 327
Middle East	
Saudi Arabia	138 667
Kuwait	75 500
Iran	60 000
Iraq	29 000
Abu Dhabi	14 850

	millions of barrels
Neutral Zone	12 800
Qatar	4 100
Oman	3 000
Syria	1 320
Dubai	1 300
Bahrein	395
Turkey	200
Israel	13
	341 145
Far East/Australasia	
Indonesia	10 000
Australia	1 661
India	743
Brunei/Malaysia	700
Burma	50
Bangladesh	35
New Zealand	26
Japan	25
Other countries	19
	13 259
USSR, Eastern Europe, China	
USSR	60 000
Eastern Europe	1 335
China	5 000
	66 335
World total	552 208

Main source reserve figures crude oil: *World Oil*, 15 August 1971

Exploration
and production (Shell)

General

In 1971, Shell companies had interests in oil and gas fields in 26 countries, producing an average of 4 526 000 b/d of crude and natural gas liquids. In addition an average of 936 000 b/d were received under special supply contracts, giving a grand total of 5 462 000 b/d.

Shell companies were also actively engaged in exploration during 1971. They were either directly exploring or had interests in exploration in 57 countries, in 27 of which exploratory drilling was undertaken.

North America

USA

In the Michigan basin, Shell Oil, on its own and in partnership, began successfully exploring Silurian carbonate rocks, about four years ago. In 1971 five commercial discoveries were made and active exploration drilling is going on. A significant discovery made in the northern Uinta basin (Utah) in 1970 was followed up in 1971 by six additional discoveries. The nature of the reservoir and the composition of the oil necessitates prolonged testing and evaluation as well as special treatment. Exploration drilling on tracts offshore Louisiana, acquired at a Federal Lease sale of December 1970, resulted in finding three commercial accumulations in 1971. During 1971 Shell Oil produced 718 700 b/d of liquid hydrocarbons (up 40 000 b/d) and 2902 MMcf/d of gas (same as 1971).

Canada

Shell Canada Limited is actively pursuing wild cat drilling in its 68·7 million acres east coast offshore permits where by end 1971, 24 wells had been drilled, but without commercial success. Exploration efforts are being continued in the Central

Plains and Foothills (Alberta and British Columbia) and activities are being substantially increased in the Northern Territories, particularly in the Mackenzie Delta area.

During 1971 Shell Canada's liquid hydrocarbons production was virtually unchanged at an average of 78 500 b/d, but sales of natural gas were higher at 488 MMcf/d.

Shell Canada and a Shell Oil Company subsidiary, Shell Explorer Limited, have concluded agreements for joint exploration and development of non-producing oil and gas interests in approximately 72 million acres of onshore and offshore concessions in Canada. The Shell Oil subsidiary is committed to spend primarily over the next six and a half years, Can$225 million for exploration work and Can$25 million for research on methods of producing synthetic crude from tar sands in Athabasca and Peace River.

For its own account Shell Canada obtained offshore exploration permits covering some 21 million acres off Baffin Island.

South and Central America

CSV's own production of crude oil and natural gas liquids in 1971 averaged 908 000 b/d compared with 935 000 b/d in 1970. This production decrease in 1971 occurred, in spite of a build-up in potential to an average of 956 000 b/d, due to market restrictions which forced CSV to close in an average of 55 000 b/d.

In Venezuela, Shell Surca, a newly established Shell company, signed a service contract with CVP, the state oil company, for the exploration and development of the 500 square kilometre Block B in south Lake Maracaibo. A seismic survey has been carried out and drilling operations are scheduled for the first half of 1972.

In Trinidad production accruing to Shell Trinidad from own operations and a one-third interest in Trinmar declined slightly to some 29 000 b/d. In late 1971 the government announced agreement in principle to the formation of a consortium (Shell interest 37·5 %) for exploration acreage off the south-east coast.

In Colombia Shell Cóndor's crude-oil production was maintained at almost 19 000 b/d in 1971, while very limited production continues in Argentina (Shell Capsa) and Peru (via Elwerath).

Exploration is proceeding at a cautious pace but on a wide front in the Caribbean where, apart from new interests in Venezuela and Trinidad, a fourth permit was secured in Honduras (offshore). Seismic surveys were made offshore Honduras and Guyana, Surinam and French Guiana. Two offshore wells drilled with partners in Guyana and Surinam were, however, abandoned but plans for further evaluation are in hand.

In South America Shell Oil (US) concluded arrangements to participate with other American oil companies in joint ventures with the national oil companies of Colombia and Peru.

Europe

During 1971 the Shell companies pursued aggressively a wide variety of exploration ventures in Western Europe. Thus Shell companies drilled on their own, or in partnership, 42 onshore and 41 offshore exploration wells which resulted in five new oil and 19 new gas discoveries. These were followed up in the same year with six appraisal wells.

Again much effort was concentrated in the North Sea area where further oil discoveries spurred industry-wide activities to a yet higher level than before.

In this context Norske Shell (Shell interest 100%) conducted extensive seismic surveys in the Norwegian offshore, evaluating open acreage and firming up locations to be drilled in 1972.

Two exploration wells drilled by the Dansk Undergrunds Consortium (Shell interest 30%) in the Danish offshore resulted in two oil discoveries. The larger one named Dan field is being developed and offshore production facilities will be installed in the first half of 1972. Initial production at a rate of 10 000 b/d is expected by end of June 1972. Crude disposal is planned by tanker from a newly installed SBM. A large seismic survey was conducted to further evaluate the area and support additional exploration drilling.

Off the Scottish coast Shell UK Exploration and Production drilling on production licences held by Shell/Esso discovered the Auk field early in 1971. Three appraisal wells drilled subsequently yielded encouraging results so that production plans are being formulated. Preparations are in hand for development of the field, which is expected to commence production in 1974. A well drilled in Shell/Esso's acreage adjoining BP's Forties oilfield discovery, demonstrated that the field extended into the Shell/Esso acreage. At the same time exploration for gas in the southern North Sea continued to meet with success.

Before the fourth round of acreage applications in August 1971, extensive seismic surveys were conducted in the North Sea as well as in the Celtic Sea and on the Atlantic Shelf west of the Shetland Islands. (In the latter two areas Shell UK operates alone.) In January 1972 Shell/Esso were awarded the two blocks in the southern North Sea for which they had applied.

In the southern North Sea, UK gas production from the Leman field at the end of 1971 amounted to some 720 MMcf/d from two platforms. Development drilling has been completed on the third platform and will commence on a fourth platform in early 1972. The Indefatigable field started regular production on 1 October and was producing at a rate of some 260 MMcf/d by end 1971. The gas is transported to shore via Leman through a trunkline laid during 1971. Further development drilling in Indefatigable is in progress.

In the Netherlands NAM's (Shell interest 50%) exploration effort for gas was rewarded with three onshore and two offshore discoveries. However, exploration for oil in the offshore was unsuccessful. On land in the Netherlands production from the Groningen gasfield at the end of 1971 was about 6000 MMcf/d, i.e. 26% more than at the end of the previous year. NAM's oil production averaged 32 100 b/d, some 3800 b/d less than the previous year.

In West Germany resumption of offshore activities was inhibited by delays in ratification of the boundary line agreement between West Germany, the Netherlands, Denmark and the UK. However, BEB's (Brigitta and Elwerath – Shell interest 50%) onshore exploration was successful in proving small additional gas reserves. BEB's gas production at the end of 1971 had risen to some 890 MMcf/d, up 22% compared with end 1970. The oil production of BEB averaged 40 800 b/d, some 1·6% less than the previous year.

In Austria RAG (Rohölgewinnungs AG – Shell interest 50%) continued exploration in Upper Austria and succeeded in proving further gas reserves.

In France exploration activities continued with seismic

surveys and drilling. Applications for additional acreage offshore and onshore have been filed.

Exploration drilling in the Spanish Mediterranean continued in Shell España/Campsa's (75% – 25%) acreage and encouraging hydrocarbon indications were obtained. Applications for several additional permits were filed in the Mediterranean.

In the Amposta field, offshore Spain, discovered in 1970, development drilling and installation of a drilling platform was commenced in late 1971. The field is scheduled to commence production in October 1972 at a rate of 30 000 b/d after production facilities and offshore bulk storage have been installed. Crude disposal will be effected by tanker from SBM.

In the Italian Adriatic Sea four new gas discoveries were made – two in Zone A (Barbara and Antonella) and two in Zone B (David and Emilio). One of these (Antonella) is in a SNIA Viscosa joint permit where Shell Italiana holds a 35% interest. The other three are in Agip/Shell Italiana permits (Shell interest 49%).

Shell Italiana acquired a $33\frac{1}{3}$% interest in three MCS (Mineraria Carbosarda) permits and a 45% interest in seven API (Anonima Petroli Italiana) permits in the Adriatic Sea.

South of Sicily surveys were carried out in the Agip/Shell Italiana permits in Zone C.

In Malta seismic surveys were carried out preparatory to exploration drilling early in 1972.

Africa

In Nigeria an intensive drilling campaign during 1971 resulted in Shell-BP Nigeria (Shell interest 50%) making several discoveries and promising extensions to existing fields on land. The oil production rate increased from about 1 000 000 b/d at the end of 1970 to 1 198 000 b/d at the end of 1971 and average annual production rose 40% from 790 000 b/d to 1 108 000 b/d.

In Gabon exploration continued on land and offshore. Seismic reconnaissance and a follow-up detail survey were carried out in the extensive Atlantic deepwater permit awarded to Shell Gabon in 1971. A second follow-up well to the offshore Lucina discovery was spudded towards the end of the year. Shell Gabon started injecting water in the Yenzi reservoir early in January 1972 as part of a large waterflood project. Production from the Gamba and Ivinga fields (Shell interest 50%) averaged 50 000 b/d.

Exploration has continued in Senegal, Ivory Coast, Cameroun, Zaire, South-West Africa, South Africa and Kenya. The remaining acreage off South-West Africa as well as the major part of the BP-Shell Kenya land acreage has been relinquished.

New exploration rights have been secured (Shell interest 100%) in Dahomey, Mauritania and Togo, whilst an agreement was concluded with Conoco in which a Shell 50% interest was obtained in extensive acreage in Chad and Niger.

In Libya the joint agreement between the National Oil Corporation and Shell Exploration (Libya) was signed on 25 July 1971 and exploration drilling started in September 1971.

Shell companies' $16\frac{2}{3}$% share of the Oasis partnership production was 137 400 b/d during 1971, with continuing limitation caused by the government's restriction on well and field production allowables. Exploration drilling has shown a sharp up-swing in response to one of the conditions imposed at the time of the 20 March price settlement.

Middle East

The Shell Company of Qatar's production averaged 207 500 b/d during 1971, from the Idd-El-Shargi and Maydan-Mahzam offshore fields. Production facilities for the new offshore Bul Hanine field, comprising a flow station, pumps, and a pipeline to Halul Island were under construction during 1971 and early 1972, and development wells are being drilled. Additional tanks, a new loading pump station and a second SBM are being constructed at the Halul Island terminal. Development drilling is in progress and the field is expected to come on stream in 1972 at a rate of 100 000 b/d.

P D (Oman)'s production (Shell interest 85%) averaged 294 300 b/d during 1971. Production in 1971 was lower than in 1970, largely due to delays in the exploration and development drilling programmes caused by the blow-out in the Yibal field which was finally controlled in June 1971. Construction work and injection well drilling for water injection schemes to improve ultimate recovery in the Fahud, Natih, and Yibal fields has been started: the influence of these projects should be felt in the next year or two. The Al Huwaisa field (discovered 1969), was brought on stream early in the year, initially at 20 000 b/d, increasing to 32 000 b/d by year end.

Turkse Shell's production during 1971 averaged 37 800 b/d. A new field was discovered at Katin, about 20 km north-east of the old Kayaköy field, thereby opening up a potentially large new area. Another possible separate oil accumulation was identified north of the Kurkan field.

Shell Hydrocarbons activities in the United Arab Emirates were wound up after drilling two dry holes, one in Sharjah and one in Umm-al Qiwain.

During 1971 Shell companies' share (14%) of the Consortium production in Iran averaged 583 600 b/d.

In 1971 Shell companies' share (23·75%) of production from the IPC companies in Iraq, Qatar and Abu Dhabi amounted to 575 400 b/d.

Far East and Australasia

In north-west Borneo (East Malaysia and Brunei) exploration and appraisal drilling in 1971 resulted in the discovery of the Bakau oilfield offshore Sarawak, in extensions to the Fairley and south-west Ampa fields offshore Brunei and oil indications offshore Sabah. Important gas discoveries were made offshore Sarawak. Development drilling boosted the crude-oil production to 239 500 b/d by the end of 1971, 93 000 b/d of which came from Sarawak fields. The new shipping terminal at Seria was taken into service at the end of the year.

In Australia Wapet's (Shell participation 28·6%) crude production from Barrow Island averaged 44 400 b/d in 1971. On Wapet's land acreage to the north of Perth gas was encountered in Walyering-1, located close to the recently-completed Dongara–Perth gas pipeline owned by West Australian Natural Gas (WANG – Shell participation 28·6%). In Burmah Oil Company of Australia's (Shell interest 16·6%) West Australia offshore acreage significant gas/condensate discoveries were made in N Rankin-1, Rankin-1, Goodwyn-1, Scott Reef-1 and Angel-1.

In New Zealand negotiations are continuing with government authorities for the supply of Maui natural gas to power stations. Production of natural gas from the Kapuni field amounted to 35 MMcf/d at the end of 1971.

In their 60 000 square kilometre concession in the Japan Sea, Nishi Nihon (Shell interest 50%) drilled two exploration wells but no significant hydrocarbons were encountered. In 1971 further areas, amounting to some 150 000 square kilometres, were applied for both in the Japan Sea and along the Pacific Coast offshore north-west Honshu and Hokkaido.

Korea Shell and Kaltim Shell (Shell interest in both 100%) continued regional seismic surveying prior to drilling planned for 1972.

Djawa Shell (Shell interest 100%) started the evaluation of the new 9500 square kilometre contract area, off the coast of South Java, while in the Java Sea Sunda Shell acquired a 28·3% interest in the eastern part of IIAPCO's south-east Sumatra contract area.

Tonga Shell, acting as operator for a consortium (Shell interest 33⅓%), drilled two wells on the Island of Tongatapu in late 1971 but no hydrocarbons were encountered.

Crude-oil production
(including natural gas liquids)

	Gross production		Net production	
			thousand b/d	
	1970	1971	1970	1971
USA	678	718	576	608
Canada	78	79	68	68
Rest of Western Hemisphere				
Venezuela	1041	1011	868	843
Trinidad	30	29	30	29
Colombia	20	19	18	17
Argentina	2	2	2	2
Peru	*	*	*	*
	1093	1061	918	891
Europe				
West Germany	21	20	21	20
Netherlands	18	16	18	16
Austria	4	4	4	4
France	*	*	*	*
UK	*	*	*	*
	43	40	43	40

* Less than one thousand barrels per day

	Gross production		Net production	
			thousand b/d	
	1970	1971	1970	1971
Africa				
Nigeria	396	554	396	554
Libya	141	137	124	120
Gabon	25	25	25	25
Algeria	44	–	38	–
	606	716	583	699
Middle East				
Iran	492	584	430	516
Iraq	349	386	309	341
Oman	332	294	291	257
Qatar	217	260	217	260
Abu Dhabi	101	137	101	137
Turkey	39	38	34	33
	1530	1699	1382	1544
Far East and Australasia				
Brunei	139	131	139	131
Malaysia	18	69	18	69
Australia	13	13	13	13
New Zealand	*	*	*	*
Bangladesh	*	*	*	*
	170	213	170	213
Total	4198	4526	3740	4063
Crude oil received under special supply contracts	937	936		

Gross production includes royalties claimable in kind; net production excludes such royalties. Both gross production and net production exclude crude oil received under special supply contracts.

* Less than one thousand barrels per day

Offshore exploration and production

The total area to the 100 fathom depth line of the continental shelves of the world covers about 11 million square miles, of which only 10% has so far been surveyed by geophysical methods. There are good prospects of finding hydrocarbons in about 20% of the total area.

Exploratory surveying and drilling is under way off the coasts of more than 90 countries; the Gulf of Mexico, the North Sea, the Mediterranean, West Africa, the Gulf and the waters around Indonesia and Australia are currently the busiest areas.

So far about 10% of the world's oil and about 5% of its natural gas production come from underwater areas adjacent to some 20 different countries. Estimated offshore proven reserves amount to some 15% of the world's total proven reserves.

The reasons for the undersea search are inherent in the long-term policies required of the industry. First, there is a need to continue to find reserves to keep pace with the future increase in demand: it has been predicted that oil demand will more than double and natural gas demand triple in the next 20 years. Secondly, apart from the need to locate and develop new reserves, there is the desirability of finding oil and gas near the large centres of population and industry.

As activity on the continental shelves has expanded it has become necessary to push the frontier of exploration beyond 100 fathoms into much deeper waters. Geophysical surveys conducted by government agencies and private industry over the past few years have indicated that thick prospective sedimentary basins extend in some cases from the continental shelves into the deep water of the oceans.

While the oil industry is already taking up exploration concessions from 100 down to 2000 fathoms, techniques are now being rapidly developed to cope with the special problems attendant on exploration, and later production, in these water depths.

For exploratory drilling at sea, mobile drilling rigs are now generally used. They can be divided into four major classes: the submersible units, the self-elevating units, both of which rest on the sea-floor, the ship-type floating rigs and the semi-submersibles or deep floaters.

The largest submersible transparent type has three main supporting members which are over 200 feet high. Each of these members terminates in a pontoon which can rest on the bottom. After drilling is completed at one location, the rig can be floated by pumping water out of the bottom hulls and ballast tanks. It can then be towed to a new location by tugs. These submersible rigs are limited, for economic reasons, to water depths of about 165 feet.

The bottom-supported, self-elevating type is generally composed of a large barge hull, on which the structure floats, and three or more legs, up to 460 feet long, which move vertically through the hull. When such a rig arrives at the drilling site it lowers its legs to the sea-floor and then elevates itself by climbing up them to a safe distance above the waves. While these self-elevating rigs are very versatile drilling tools, they are expensive to build, difficult to move from one drilling location to another, and are limited to water depths of approximately 300 feet. They have to resist the forces experienced while resting on the sea-floor and the strains caused by the ocean swell when they are floating.

Much of the pioneering and development work on floating drilling was started as long ago as 1948 by the CUSS group, in which a Shell company played a significant role, and which led to the development of the drillship *Cuss I* which was held on location by a system of anchors.

Although a ship can move fast between successive drilling locations, it experiences severe motions in rough seas which interfere with the progress of the drilling operation. Shell scientists and engineers therefore undertook research in the late 1950s and after exhaustive tests of models in wave tanks developed a deep-floating structure in which the drilling platform is supported by an open or transparent type of structure floating on buoyancy chambers placed well below the zone of wave action (30 to 80 feet below the surface). It was found that such a semi-submersible unit would be considerably more stable than ship-shaped units.

In 1961, a Shell company was the first to apply this principle by converting a bottom-supported transparent type rig to a semi-submersible unit. The success of this prototype led to the building of many such structures, one of which is the Shell-designed and owned *Staflo* which has been operating for the past four years in the hostile environment of the North Sea. In addition, Shell companies, which taken together constitute the largest offshore operators, now have, in addition to ten bottom-supported jack-up units and three drilling vessels, some eight contractor-owned semi-submersibles under contract in various parts of the world.

At present more than 20 semi-submersibles are being built at yards in Europe and the USA. Almost all of these are designed to withstand extreme weather conditions, such as for example, waves of up to 100 feet in height. They have a displacement of 20 000 tons or more in the drilling position and many of them are self-propelled. The cost of these new types is around £8 million each, including the drilling equipment. Shell UK Exploration and Production has three of these units under contract which will operate in the rough weather areas of the northern North Sea.

The conventional anchoring system has permitted drilling in almost 1000 feet of water. In deeper water these anchoring systems become very expensive and are extremely time-consuming to handle. For these reasons, a method known as dynamic stationing has been conceived for keeping vessels on location without the use of anchors; here the tendency for the drilling vessel to move under wind, wave and current forces is counteracted by using computer-controlled propulsion units placed in opposite positions around the vessel. Such a system was first used in 1961 when it was installed on the drilling vessel *Cuss I* for drilling in over 10 000 feet of water for Phase I of the Mohole Project.

During 1970 construction work was started on three dynamically-stationed drillships, each having a displacement of about 15 000 tons in drilling condition. One of them, the *Sedco 445*, has recently been commissioned and is under a long-term contract to SIPC. Two main screws provide the longitudinal thrust of 80 000 to 120 000 lb, while 11 fixed axis, fixed pitch propellers with Kort nozzles can provide a lateral thrust of about 220 000 lb to keep the vessel over the drilling location without the use of chains and anchors.

Floating drilling requires a flexible conduit, from the moving rig to the fixed point on the ocean floor, which cannot be made to withstand high pressures, and has led to the development of underwater wellheads and blow-out preventer stacks. This equipment, installed just above the sea bottom, is what has inspired the expression 'underwater drilling'. These blow-out preventer assemblies are up to 35 feet high, weigh up to 75 tons and have a working pressure of up to 10 000 psi. Their installation and operation is remote-controlled from the surface.

Development drilling

When the geophysical surveys and exploratory drilling have indicated that oil or gas has been discovered in commercial quantities, the development of the field with permanent platforms begins. In many cases fixed platforms can be used. They must be designed to remain in position for 25 to 40 years, the normal life span of an oilfield, and from them as many as 30 directional wells may be drilled to reach the producing formation. These wells can be deviated from the vertical and several thousand feet horizontally from the platform.

There are two primary types of permanent drilling platform: the tender-assisted and the self-contained. In the former type the platform itself supports only a small part of the drilling equipment. An adjacent tender supports the remainder of the equipment, the supplies and the quarters for the drilling crews.

The self-contained platform is designed to support a complete drilling rig, the drilling supplies and quarters for 50 to 60 men. This is the primary development tool available to Shell companies, and has been used in offshore locations throughout the world in up to some 400 feet of water.

Offshore production

The production phase of offshore operations involves installing treating, storage and transportation facilities. The chief function of the treating facilities is to remove water and separate gas from oil or condensates from gas.

In relatively shallow water, nowadays considered to be up to some 400 feet, these facilities are placed on platforms, together with all ancillary facilities for accommodating the required operations personnel, and special equipment, such as pollution control devices and gas flaring facilities, etc.

For transporting oil from offshore locations either tankers

or pipelines are used, depending on the economics of the situation. Normally a pipeline is preferred, as it will simplify operations; however, the depth of water encountered or the long distance to shore might in some cases prohibit the construction of a pipeline on the grounds of cost. Together with the offshore production facilities, other installations required for the economic exploitation of the reservoir, such as water or gas injection facilities, are incorporated in the total development of an offshore field.

Marine structure construction. The technology of marine construction calls for skilled men and special facilities to fabricate and weld steel plates up to two inches or more in thickness, to erect large steel sections up to 250 feet in height, and install structures weighing 8000 tons in water 400 feet deep. For these installations a construction barge is used, normally equipped with a 250 to 600 ton revolving crane, and which, together with its crew and assisting tugs, may cost up to £10 000/day.

Sea-floor drilling and production. As exploration and drilling activities have gone into deeper water, the permanent platforms required for supporting the drilling and production equipment have become increasingly expensive. A structure in 50 feet of water may cost £500 000; in 300 feet costs of up to £2 million may be expected in severe conditions. Preliminary designs indicate that in 600 feet of water a structure may cost £10 million. Fixed platforms will begin to reach the end of their usefulness as progress is made into even greater depths of water. Great progress has been made in developing new techniques for placing wells in deep water using floating drilling rigs and wells can now be completed by remote control from the surface with underwater wellhead equipment. Production of hydrocarbons from sea bed wells will also require the use of new techniques and Shell engineers are actively developing production systems using floating platforms and deep water tanker loading methods.

At the end of 1971 there were 240 offshore drilling units operating and more than 50 under construction. In addition, equipment and techniques have been developed for divers to operate in water depths of up to about 700 feet.

Natural gas (World)

General properties

The principal constituent of natural gas is methane. Volume for volume, it has about twice the heating value of manufactured gas. Its special characteristics of cleanliness, ease of combustion control and the absence of contaminants make it an ideal low-pollution fuel with a wide range of high-grade industrial applications in addition to its established uses for domestic cooking and heating.

Natural gas is also a useful feedstock for making hydrogen for ammonia and nitrogenous fertilizer production. Certain plastics and synthetic fibres and other chemicals can also be made from the methane molecule, but in general natural gas is not such a good chemical feedstock as the unsaturated petroleum gases, e.g. ethylene, propylene and butylene.

Reserves terminology

Natural gas is found in underground structures similar to those containing crude oil and from the production viewpoint may be placed in two main categories viz:

(a) Associated gas – from reservoirs where gas is found dissolved in crude oil (solution gas) or in contact with gas-saturated crude (gas-cap gas). Gas production rates depend on oil output.

(b) Non-associated gas – either from structures capable of producing only gas economically or from condensate reservoirs which yield relatively large amounts of gas per barrel of light liquid hydrocarbons.

Natural gas may also be referred to either as 'wet', implying that it still contains certain quantities of the heavier hydrocarbons (ethane, propane, butane etc), or 'dry', which means that it has been processed to remove these components, (*see* natural gas liquids, on page 80).

Natural gas liquids (NGL)

Not to be confused with liquefied natural gas or LNG (*see* page 81 under Transportation). Gas liquids comprise those hydrocarbons which can be extracted in liquid form from natural gas as produced. They can be further classified into the following two categories:

Liquefied petroleum gases (LPG)

Normally gaseous but easily liquefied by cooling or compression and comprising mainly propane and butane with the unsaturated fractions (propylene and butylene) being present only in very small proportions.

Natural gasoline (Casinghead gasoline)

A liquid product under normal conditions consisting variously of the heavier hydrocarbons (pentanes $+$) extracted from field gas by compression, absorption etc and suitable for use as a blending component.

Units of measurement

Gas is measured usually either in cubic feet (ft^3) or cubic metres (m^3), production and sales volumes being quoted in terms of milliard (thousand million) m^3 annually or million ft^3 daily (MMcf/d), depending on the country concerned. Approximate equivalents are as follows:

1 mrd m^3 per year	$=100$ MMcf/d
	$=900\ 000$ tons fuel oil per year
	$=1\ 400\ 000$ tons coal per year
	$=17\ 600$ barrels oil per day
	$=700\ 000$ tons liquefied natural gas per year
1 barrel oil	$=5800\ ft^3/154\ m^3$ natural gas
1 ton of oil	$=43\ 000\ ft^3/1150\ m^3$ natural gas
1 ton liquefied natural gas (LNG)	$=15$ barrels liquid
	$=1400\ m^3$ pipeline gas
	$=53\ 000\ ft^3$ pipeline gas

The above conversions are based on natural gas with a

calorific value of 9500 kcal/m³, approximately equal to 1000 Btu/ft³. Not all natural gases, however, are equal in this respect. For example, gas from Groningen in the Netherlands contains 14% of nitrogen and has therefore a somewhat lower calorific value of 8400 kcal/m³ (880 Btu/ft³); 30 m³ Groningen gas = 1 million Btu = 10 therms.

Natural gas reserves

The following table lists proven reserves of both associated and non-associated gas. The figures should be taken as broad indications of orders of magnitude only.

	mrd m³		mrd m³
USA/Mexico	7 950	Middle East	9 750
Canada	1 550	Africa	5 450
Central and		Far East	2 000
South America	1 750	USSR, Eastern Europe	
Western Europe	4 600	and China	15 800

Natural gas production 1970

	mrd m³		mrd m³
USA/Mexico	627	Middle East	86
Canada	75	Africa	48
Central and		Far East	18
South America	74	USSR, Eastern Europe	
Western Europe	84	and China	237

Transportation

The use of large-diameter steel pipelines, working at high pressure, to link gasfields and consuming areas on land is a well-established feature of the natural gas industry. The underlying technology was developed very largely to meet the conditions of the North American market where in general the producing areas are located away from the main centres of demand and where the key to large-scale gas utilisation at competitive prices lay in establishing the facilities for economical bulk transport over the long distances

F

involved. Outside the USA also, much use has subsequently been made of this form of transportation in areas with natural gas reserves, notably in recent years the USSR, continental Europe and the UK.

To complement these overland transfers by pipeline, considerable interest is now being shown in moving natural gas by sea as a means of using the surplus reserves or production which occur in certain areas of the world to meet deficits arising elsewhere. To this end, the gas can first be liquefied by cooling to minus 161°C (minus 258°F) at atmospheric pressure down to one six-hundredth of its original volume and then shipped in special insulated tankers to storage and regasification terminals located in or near the main centres of consumption.

The first commercial movement of this nature was developed by Conch International Methane for the delivery of the liquid equivalent of about 1 mrd m³ per annum from Algeria to the UK starting in 1964, while a parallel scheme supplies about half this quantity annually from the same source to north-west France. Other developments have followed and movements of LNG are now operational between Alaska and Japan, Libya and Italy/Spain with occasional shipments from Algeria to the US eastern seaboard market. Two further projects, Brunei/Japan and Algeria/southern France, are expected to become operational this year. A number of other schemes are under study in various parts of the world, including possible deliveries into Japan from Australia/ Sarawak/Middle East and large-scale movements into the USA from the Caribbean, Nigeria and North Africa.

Natural gas (Shell)

Shell companies have an important share of world gas reserves and a large and growing stake in gas utilisation. They marketed a total of 54·1 mrd m³ in 1971, 12% up on 1970.

Australia

West Australian Petroleum (Shell participation 28·6%) at the end of 1971 commenced deliveries of gas to the Perth area via a new 260-mile 14-inch pipeline from its Dongara gasfield. There is a 16·7% Shell interest in gas discoveries made in 1971 off the north-western coast. The extent of these discoveries and their development prospects have yet to be fully appraised.

Bangladesh

Deliveries of gas by Shell Oil Company (Shell interest 75%) from the Titas field to Dacca via the Titas Gas Company (Shell interest 10%) began in 1968 as did sales from Habiganj to a neighbouring new power station. Total sales from these two fields reached only 0·2 mrd m³ in 1971, compared with 0·4 mrd m³ in 1970, due to local hostilities interrupting deliveries.

Belgium

Market demand for natural gas is wholly met by imports from the Netherlands under long-term contracts between NAM and the Belgian distributing company, Distrigaz, in which Shell and Esso together have each a one-sixth participation. The conversion of the public distribution system to natural gas has almost been completed. Deliveries of Dutch gas in 1971 were 6·3 mrd m³ compared with 4·5 mrd m³ in 1970.

Canada

Shell Canada sold 4·8 mrd m³ natural gas in 1971, an increase of 12% over the previous year.

Denmark
Natural gas discoveries have been announced by Dansk Undergrunds Consortium (Shell interest 30%) in the Danish sector of the North Sea but these have not yet been evaluated.

France
Gaz de France, which has a virtual monopoly of gas sales, purchases NAM gas at the Dutch border and Distrigaz arranges transit through Belgium and delivery at the Franco-Belgian border. Supplies of Dutch gas totalled 4·4 mrd m³ in 1971 compared with 3·0 mrd m³ in 1970, representing about 35% of the total natural gas consumed in France.

Italy
Total reserves are estimated to be around 200 mrd m³ with approximately one-third in the Adriatic offshore area. The Shell share of three small commercial fields so far discovered in that area by a joint Shell/AGIP exploration venture was sold to ENI. Agreement has been signed between NAM and ENI for deliveries of Dutch gas at the Dutch border starting in 1974 and rising to over 6 mrd m³ per year.

From the planned Netherlands/Italy trunkline system, about 0·5 mrd m³ per year of NAM gas will eventually be delivered to Switzerland.

Japan
An important development in 1970 was the signature of contracts between a Shell/Mitsubishi company and three Japanese customers, Tokyo Electric, Tokyo Gas and Osaka Gas, covering the supply of 65 million tons of LNG from Brunei over a 20-year period, with initial deliveries being made in the winter of 1972–3. This was followed in February 1972 by a further agreement with the same customers for an additional 25 million tons of LNG from Brunei for delivery over 20 years commencing in 1973. Shell interests in the project as a whole are: production (Brunei Shell Petroleum – Shell interest 100%), liquefaction (Brunei LNG Ltd – Shell interest 45%), and trading (Coldgas Trading Ltd – Shell interest 50%).

The complete chain of facilities (production, liquefaction, loading and shipping) is designed to deliver annually the equivalent of just over 5 million tons of LNG. The project will call for the employment of seven 75 000 m³ capacity LNG tankers, all of which have been ordered by Shell Tankers UK Ltd who will charter them to Coldgas Trading Ltd.

The Netherlands

Recoverable reserves in the Netherlands are now assessed at about 2400 mrd m³, the bulk of which is concentrated in the Groningen field in the northern part of the country, discovered in 1959 by NV Nederlandse Aardolie Mij (NAM – Shell and Esso interests 50% each). NAM is the concession holder and produces Groningen gas on behalf of a financial partnership, the 'Maatschap', in which NAM holds a 60% interest and the Dutch State Mines 40%. NV Nederlandse Gasunie (10% Netherlands Government, 40% State Mines, Shell and Esso interests 25% each) purchases gas from the Maatschap for transport and sale to large industrial users and municipalities within the Netherlands, while export contracts are negotiated by a specialist division of NAM, with the proceeds of such sales at the border accruing to Gasunie.

In 1971, NAM sales of Dutch natural gas totalled 43·5 mrd m³ (compared with 31·4 mrd m³ in the previous year) of which 26·3 mrd m³ (60%) represented sales within the Netherlands and 17·2 mrd m³ (40%) exports, of which, in turn 38% went to West Germany, 36% to Belgium and 26% to France. By 1976, about 50% of the Netherlands total energy requirements is expected to be met by natural gas.

New Zealand

Sales of natural gas from Shell BP and Todd's Kapuni field (Shell interest 37·5%) to the state natural gas corporation which commenced in 1970 rose to 0·15 mrd m³ in 1971.

In 1969, Shell BP and Todd (Shell interest 37·5%) discovered the Maui gas and condensate field some 30 miles off the south-west coast of the North Island. Negotiations continue for the sale of this gas to the state national gas corporation, principally for power generation purposes.

Nigeria

Shell-BP Nigeria (Shell interest 50%) has discovered natural gas reserves in quantities which far exceed the requirements of the local market. Evaluations are therefore currently being made to assess the prospects for exporting substantial volumes of this gas as LNG, with the east coast of the United States figuring as the principal market of interest.

Sarawak
Following the discovery by Shell Sarawak of offshore natural gas reserves, the prospects for an LNG export scheme to Japan are being investigated.

Trinidad
Shell Trinidad's sales were 0·51 mrd m³ in 1971, 14% up on 1970.

United Kingdom
Reserves of natural gas in the British sector of the North Sea are estimated to be between 750–850 mrd m³ (excluding the unquantified discoveries in the northern region) of which some 14% is owned jointly by Shell/Esso. The total sales of natural gas in 1971 were some 20 mrd m³ against 12 mrd m³ in 1970. The Shell share of sales in 1971 from the Leman and Indefatigable fields (the latter commenced production at the end of 1971) was 2·8 mrd m³, a 65% increase over the 1970 level of 1·7 mrd m³.

USA
Shell Oil's natural gas sales of 27·0 mrd m³ in 1971 were broadly in line with those of 1970.

West Germany
Continuing exploration has increased indigenous reserves to the point where they now amount to some 400 mrd m³ of which about one-half is collectively owned by Brigitta and Elwerath, companies in which there is a 50% Shell interest, which delivered a total of 8·8 mrd m³ in 1971 or some 60% of total indigenous West German production, compared with 7 mrd m³ (58%) in 1970.

Dutch gas imports contributed a further 6·5 mrd m³ or about 28% of total West German consumption in 1971. Based mainly on contracts made by NAM with Thyssengas (Shell interest 25%) and Ruhrgas (total Shell holding 15%) and an additional contract with Brigitta, Dutch imports are expected to reach about 40% of total consumption by 1976.

There are also Shell interests ranging from 20% to 32% in three West German pipeline companies engaged in the transport of mainly Dutch gas from the Netherlands border to various distributing companies as far south as Mannheim.

Under agreements signed by Ruhrgas in 1969 and 1971, imports of Soviet gas into southern Germany are expected to commence in 1973 building up progressively to a level of some 5·0 mrd m³ by about 1976.

Venezuela
CSV's sales in 1971 were 1·0 mrd m³, much the same level as in 1970.

Marine (World)

The world tanker and combined carrier fleet at 1 January 1972 comprised some 4481 ships (2000 dwt and over), totalling 195·8 million tons deadweight.* This consisted of:

4225 tankers	173·5 million dwt
256 combination carriers	22·3 million dwt

Oil companies owned 27% of the fleet by deadweight, independent owners 67% and the remaining 6% was owned by governments.

Classification by deadweight

	Number	million dwt	%
Under 16 500	1242	8·6	4·4
16 500–25 000	1024	20·3	10·3
25 000–45 000	857	28·9	14·8
45 000–80 000	712	42·8	21·9
80 000–160 000	408	42·7	21·8
Over 160 000	238	52·5	26·8
	4481	195·8	100·0

Classification by Flag

	% (dwt)	Approx million dwt		% (dwt)	Appox million dwt
Liberian	24·5	47·6	Panamanian	3·5	6·8
British	15·0	29·2			
Norwegian	11·1	21·3		79·4	154·0
Japanese	10·2	19·8	Other flags	20·6	41·8
USA	5·7	11·1			
Greek	5·2	10·1		100·0	195·8
French	4·2	8·1			

* Deadweight tonnage (dwt) – weight of cargo, stores, bunkers and water that a ship can carry expressed in tons of 2240 lb

The average age of the world tanker and combination carrier fleet is 13 years. The VLCC class of vessel which represents 26·8% of the total deadweight capacity has an average age of less than three years. The first VLCCs were delivered in 1967.

New buildings

At the end of 1971 the world's tanker order book consisted of 525 tankers with a total of 89 million dwt. Oil company orders accounted for 40% by deadweight. In addition, there were orders for 141 combination carriers with a total tonnage of 21 million dwt. The total orders represent an increase of 22% on the order book as at year-end 1970.

Tanker new building orders at the end of 1971 represented approximately 55% of the total gross register tonnage* on order at that time.

The largest tanker and combination carrier on order are 477 000 dwt and 269 500 dwt respectively.

Some approximate tanker data:

dwt	Building cost £m	Full loaded draught		Length overall		Typical annual cargo tons	Gross tonnage
		ft	(m)	ft	(m)		
24 000	4·0	32·5	(9·9)	580	(171)	120 000	15 000
120 000	9·0	52·0	(15·9)	885	(270)	655 000	63 000
300 000	18·0	73·0	(22·7)	1132	(345)	1 656 000	150 000

Building yards

At June 1970 Japanese yards had obtained 50% of all new orders for tanker tonnage and 56% of all combined carrier tonnage, whereas European yards secured 47% and 44% respectively.

Ship building capacity tends to increase, especially in terms of berths for VLCCs. It has been reported that by 1975 the building capacity of Japanese yards is likely to be in excess of the present total world output. Increased facilities for building large vessels have recently become available in Spain.

Freight rates

Worldscale. The objective of Worldscale is to furnish a list of basic freight rates for all voyages upon which tankers ply. The

* Gross register tonnage (grt) – total capacity of all enclosed spaces in ships, measured in 'tons' of 100 cubic ft (ft³)

rates are calculated by taking into account the particular characteristics of each voyage, and by using a common set of assumptions. This provides a schedule of rates calculated to a common base which accurately reflects the relationship between one voyage and another.

The basic Worldscale rate provides a reference value for the freight level for a particular route. It is not intended to express operational costs. The actual freight level for a particular route will depend on the state of the market.

Average freight rate assessment

AFRA provides a factual average of rates being paid for tankers during any one month. The rate is calculated by using all current commercial charter rates, i.e. long, short term and single voyage fixtures, which apply to tankers in international trade. It therefore reflects the overall average rate for all chartered tanker tonnage at any given time. Separate calculations are made for varying size ranges of vessels and are published in terms of the Worldscale Freight Schedule.

The AFRA levels are produced monthly by an independent body, the London Brokers Panel.

Environmental considerations

Companies within the tanker and oil industries have entered into two voluntary agreements concerning the liability for pollution damage. These ensure that governments and persons, anywhere in the world, who suffer damage from oil pollution caused by a tanker are reimbursed and compensated fairly and promptly.

The first agreement is TOVALOP (Tanker Owners' Voluntary Agreement concerning Liability for Oil Pollution). This concerns the liability of tanker owners for pollution damage and involves payments to governments. The second agreement is CRISTAL (Contract Regarding an Interim Supplement to Tanker Liability for Oil Pollution). This acts as a supplement to TOVALOP. Subscriptions are paid by oil companies. Compensation can be paid to individuals as well as governments.

For every tanker ordered after 1971 there will be a limit on the maximum volume of any one tank. The purpose of this regulation, formulated by IMCO (International Maritime

Consultative Organisation), is to limit the outflow of oil from a tanker following an accident.

Operations

The trend towards operating larger vessels continues. The largest vessel in service, a tanker, is the 372 698 dwt *Nisseki Maru*.

Crude oil carriers of 100 000–160 000 dwt discharge, under good conditions, about 7000–8000 mt of oil per hour, whereas VLCCs are capable of pumping up to 16 000 m³ per hour.

At any given time approximately 70 million tons of oil is being moved by the world tanker and combination carrier fleet.

An average speed of 15·5 knots is fairly representative of tankers over 25 000 dwt (1 knot = 1 nautical mile (6080 ft or 1852 m) per hour).

Routes

Lengths of the major tanker routes in nautical miles are approximately:

The Middle East Gulf–NW Europe	11 600
The Middle East Gulf–Japan	6 700
West Africa–NW Europe	4 700
Libya–NW Europe	2 450
Caribbean–United States	1 800
Caribbean–NW Europe	4 200

Gas carriers

The market for the transportation of LNG is relatively new but a potential exists for a high rate of expansion. This has led to a growth in LNG tanker construction.

At the end of 1971 there were 13 LNG tankers in service with a combined capacity of 478 000 m³. It has been reported that to meet envisaged future demands for tonnage about twice as many vessels of varying sizes with a total capacity of 2 044 000 m³ have been ordered for delivery between 1972 and 1977. The largest of these vessels, due for delivery in 1975, has a capacity of 125 000 m³.

Marine (Shell)

At 31 December 1971 tankers owned and managed by Shell operating companies totalled 190 vessels, (2000 dwt and over), aggregating 10·2 million dwt, which is 5·3% of the world tanker tonnage.

Distribution of the fleet, by company, was as follows:

Company	Vessels	dwt
Compañía Shell de Venezuela	6	151 525
Deutsche Shell Tanker	11	803 832
Shell Compañía Argentina de Petróleo SA	8	153 172
Shell Canada Limited	6	86 374
Shell Tankers (UK) Ltd	86	5 280 657
Shell Tankers NV	52	2 223 264
Shell Sempaku kk	2	241 843
Société Maritime Shell	13	1 241 793
Société Angkor	1	2 122
Shell International Marine	1	24 772
Shell-Mex and BP	4	8 884
	190	10 218 238

The average age (by numbers of ships) of the owned Shell fleet is 12·3 years: that of the Shell owned VLCCs is 3·0 years.

Vessels time chartered by Shell companies total 253 of 16·4 million dwt. The total fleet of Shell owned and chartered vessels at the end of 1971 comprised 443 vessels of 26·6 million dwt, approximately 13·7% of the total world tanker and combination carrier tonnage.

Classification by deadweight.

	No	Owned thousands dwt	No	Chartered thousands dwt
Under 16 500	20	153	18	154
16 500–25 000	73	1 389	54	1 086
25 000–45 000	29	1 000	51	1 627
45 000–80 000	38	2 376	67	4 297
80 000–160 000	9	983	39	3 966
Over 160 000	21	4 318	24	5 301
Total	190	10 219	253	16 431

Included in the above figures are 16 chartered combination carriers trading for Shell companies in oil, total 1·58 million dwt.

By the end of 1971 45 owned and chartered ships over 160 000 dwt were in service with Shell companies.

The flag analysis of the Shell fleet, both owned and chartered, is as follows:

	No	Owned % (dwt)	No	Chartered % (dwt)
British	90	51	26	9
Norwegian	—	—	62	32
Liberian	8	4	64	26
Dutch	44	20	7	1
Japanese	2	2	12	7
French	14	11	2	1
West German	11	7	2	1
	169	95	175	77
Others	21	5	78	23
	190	100	253	100

New buildings

To provide for future tonnage requirements the following tankers were on order at 1 January, 1972.

Class	No	Years of delivery	Approx dwt	Total dwt
Product carriers	9	1974–1976	32 000	288 000
VLCCs	27	1972–1976	250 000–310 000	7 807 000
	36			8 095 000

The product carriers on order will replace ships that are approaching obsolescence with present ages of up to 18 years.

The VLCCs under construction are part of Shell companies second major new building programme in this class.

Operations

Throughout the world over 10 000 people are employed within the Marine function. This includes 2300 personnel employed on a non-contract basis. New patterns of manning on Shell vessels concerning the re-allocation and interchangeability of manpower have led to an overall increase in operational efficiency. This has been assisted by the introduction of increased maintenance and more sophisticated equipment.

The flexibility of VLCCs has been greatly increased by the use of two 'lightening' vessels. At present it is planned to introduce another larger vessel of this type.

On any given day Shell tanker fleets are moving some 10 million tons of oil. This includes crude oil, feedstocks and products. In all there are about 100 ocean supply points and 350 discharging points that are used worldwide by the Shell fleet.

Main hauls are from the major crude-oil loading terminals in the Middle East, West and North Africa and Eastern Mediterranean, to the refineries of north-west Europe, southern France and Italy, the Far East, Australia and Japan; from the Caribbean to North America and across the North and South Atlantic. There are also significant movements from Malaysia, Brunei and Indonesia to Australia and Japan.

Tovalop and Cristal

Members of the Royal Dutch/Shell Group of Companies were among the original sponsors of Tovalop and all Shell operating companies which transport oil by sea, or which receive oil at their terminals, are members of Cristal. All Shell owned vessels and nearly all the vessels chartered are entered in Tovalop.

Gas carriers

For the past eight years Shell Tankers (UK) has managed two methane ships of 27 500 m^3 capacity. These have been employed carrying Algerian gas to the United Kingdom.

Shell Tankers (UK) now has on order seven LNG vessels each with 75 000 m^3 capacity. These are scheduled for delivery from 1972–75 and will be dedicated to the Brunei LNG Project serving customers in Tokyo and Osaka.

Pipelines (World)

Pipelines were originally used almost entirely for transporting crude oil from the producing field to tanker terminal or directly to refineries. Now the pipeline is becoming more and more a transporter of energy, since the crude-oil function has been complemented by product pipelines from refineries and a phenomenal increase in natural-gas transmission and distribution lines as more nations every year convert to natural gas. To these three mainstays of the pipeline industry other types of pipeline have been added in recent years. Typical examples are LPG lines distributing propane and butane, ethylene, propylene and slurry lines; other lines foreseen in the not-too-distant future include liquefied-natural-gas and coal-gas pipelines, which are both under serious study.

The role of pipelines in the energy picture is highlighted by these facts:

– there are more than 1 million miles of trunk and gathering pipelines in the world; about 70% of this mileage is natural-gas pipeline, some 20% crude and the remainder products pipelines and other energy pipelines.

– in 1971 some 15 000 miles of trunk and gathering pipelines were constructed.

– much of the new construction is in large-diameter sizes (30, 36, 42 inches).

– submarine pipeline activity is spreading to even deeper waters in order to bring ashore crude and gas production from new offshore fields.

– the ever increasing number of VLCCs means increasing demand for larger diameter sea loading and unloading lines around the world.

– big chemical companies are interlinking their plants by pipeline.

Economics

Pipeline economics are characterized by large investments, relatively low operating costs, and decreasing unit cost for higher volumes. A typical cost curve for a pipeline with a given diameter brings out the fact that the fixed element in the unit transportation cost (i.e. mainly capital charges on initial investment) is high compared with variable costs. (Graph No 1.)

In contrast to other forms of transport, pipeline operations require little labour. The substantial elements in variable costs are the additional capital charges for pumps and the energy needed for higher flow rates, especially in later years. The graphs show that costs increase as throughputs exceed or fall below the 'optimum', that is the throughput at which the total unit cost reaches the lowest point.

The cost of building a pipeline of a given length is approximately proportional to the diameter of the pipe and depends upon the kind of terrain and the skill and manpower available. As volume rises the investment per ton of capacity decreases. In view of the importance of 'fixed costs', large throughputs generally mean lower unit transportation costs. Graph No 2 shows this basic economic fact for various pipeline sizes.

This is the reason why oil companies, competing in other fields, tend to join together in building pipelines. Their combined throughputs often justify a larger line, so that transportation costs are reduced all round.

Choosing the most economic line means selecting the diameter that will provide the lowest unit transportation costs over the expected life of the pipeline. Since pipelines have an economic life of twenty years or more, there has to be pretty accurate long-term forecasting.

Shippers pay a tariff for the transportation and other services (e.g. storage) performed by a pipeline company. The tariff covers operating and maintenance costs, interest on borrowed capital, depreciation, taxes and profit.

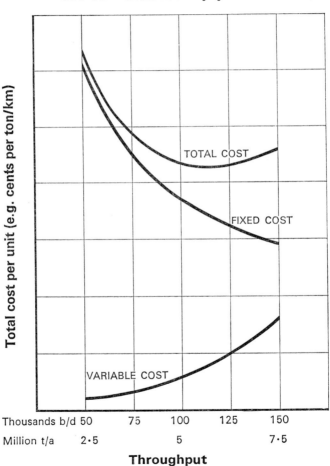

1 Transportation cost for 16″ diameter pipeline

TOTAL COST

FIXED COST

VARIABLE COST

Total cost per unit (e.g. cents per ton/km)

| Thousands b/d | 50 | 75 | 100 | 125 | 150 |
| Million t/a | 2·5 | | 5 | | 7·5 |

Throughput

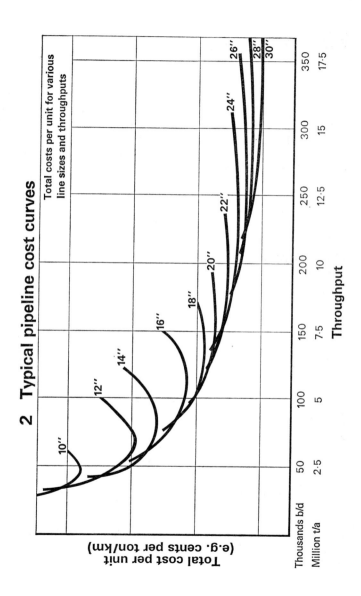

2 Typical pipeline cost curves

Total costs per unit for various line sizes and throughputs

Pipelines (Shell)

In 1971 Shell companies acquired or participated in the building of 3300 miles of pipeline in various parts of the world. Shell companies now own or have an interest in 51 650 miles of crude-oil, oil products and natural-gas pipelines, some of which are listed below:

	Length	Diameter	Capacity	Company
	miles	inches	thousands b/d	
North America				
Crude oil (Canada/USA)				
Edmonton – Vancouver – Ferndale – Anacortes (USA)	718	24	400	Trans-Mountain Pipeline
Portland (Maine) – Montreal	236×3	24/18/12	400	Portland-Montreal Pipeline
Edmonton – Chicago – Sarnia – Port Credit (Ontario) – Buffalo (NY)	2025	16/34	1100	Interprovincial Pipeline Lakehead Pipeline
Crude oil (USA)				
Louisiana – Patoka (Illinois)	635	40	497	Capline
Cushing (Oklahoma) – Wood River refinery (Illinois)	433	22	280	Ozark Pipeline

	Length	Diameter	Capacity	Company
	miles	inches	thousands b/d	
Aneth (Utah) – Wilmington refinery, Los Angeles (Calif)	670	16	80	Four Corners Pipeline
McCamey (Texas) – Houston refinery	455	24	250	Rancho Pipeline

Oil products (USA)

	Length	Diameter	Capacity	Company
Wood River refinery to terminals in Illinois, Indiana and Ohio	350	12/8	86	East Products Pipeline
Wood River refinery to terminals in Illinois and East Chicago (Ind)	260	14	100	North Products Pipeline
Ferndale and Anacortes refineries (Wash) – Seattle – Tacoma – Portland (Oregon)	312	16/14	115	Olympic Pipeline

South America
Crude oil (Venezuela)

	Length	Diameter	Capacity	Company
Palmarejo – Cardón	160	30/20	325	CSV
Anaco – Pto La Cruz	61	30/36/16	800	Meneg
Oficina – Anaco	35	30/16	700	Meneg

	Length	Diameter	Capacity	Company
	miles	inches	thousands b/d	

Western Europe
Crude oil

	Length	Diameter	Capacity	Company
Europoort (Netherlands) – Wesel – Godorf and Raunheim refineries (West Germany)	300	36/24	460	Rotterdam Rijn Pijpleiding Mij (RRP)
Lavéra – Strasbourg (France) – Karlsruhe (West Germany)	490	34	700	Société du Pipe-line Sud-Européen (SPLSE)
Fos – Lyon	160	24	150	
Trieste (Italy) – Ingolstadt (West Germany)	290	40	700	Transalpine Pipeline (TAL)
Ingolstadt – Karlsruhe	180	26	350	Rhein-Donau Oelleitung (RDO)
Wuermlach-Schwechat (Austria)	260	18	120	Adria-Wien Pipeline (AWP)

Oil products

	Length	Diameter	Capacity	Company
Le Havre – Paris	395	10/12/20	340	Trapil
Pernis (Netherlands) – Dinslaken (West Germany)	130	24	270	Rhein-Main Rohrleitungs Transport Gesellschaft
Dinslaken-Godorf	75	20	260	
Godorf-Ludwigshafen	110	20	200	(RMR)
La Mède – Fos – Lyon – Swiss border	365	16/12/10	120	Société du Pipeline Méditerranée Rhône (SPMR)
Thames – Mersey	245	14/12/10	80	United Kingdom Oil Pipelines (UKOP)

	Length	Diameter	Capacity	Company
	miles	inches	thousands b/d	
Natural gas				
Netherlands main system	1 120	48/42/36 30/24	–	Nederlandse Gasunie (NGU)
West Germany main system	163	40/36/32	–	Nordrheinische Erdgas Transport GmbH (NETG)
	107	36	–	Mittelrheinische Erdgas Transport GmbH (METG)

Middle East
Crude oil

Oman Fahud – Mina-al-Fahal	177	30/32/36	385	Petroleum Development (Oman)
Iran Marun – Ganaveh	155	36/42		
Gachsaran – Ganaveh	60	26/30	4000	ICEPC
Ganaveh – Kharg Island	30	30/42		

North Africa
Crude oil

Libya Gialo – Waha – Es Sider	400	24/30/32	1050	Oasis

Highlights

In the US, pipeline systems owned and operated by Shell Pipe Line Corporation delivered over 2 million barrels a day of crude and petroleum products in 1971. This is a 10% increase over 1970 and is almost double the amount delivered in 1966.

Construction projects either under way or finished in 1971 by Shell Pipe Line totalled over $18 million.

About $4 million was spent expanding the Capline system. This included expansion of the St James terminal on the Gulf of Mexico to enable it to receive ocean going tankers, increasing pump capacities at four stations and constructing additional tanks. The 40-inch diameter 635-mile Capline system (Shell interest 12%) now has a carrying capacity of approximately 500 000 b/d and is the largest crude-oil pipeline in the US.

Another $4 million was spent to install a 22-inch diameter loop line and meter change out on the Shell operated Ship Shoal system, thereby increasing the capacity of the system from 140 000 b/d to almost 200 000 b/d. Ship Shoal (Shell interest 42·5%) delivers offshore Louisiana crude to a shore terminal at Gibson and also supplies crude to Capline at the St James terminal.

Construction of the 1300-mile Explorer products pipeline (Shell interest approx 25%) was completed in late 1971. The line runs from the Texas Gulf coast to the Chicago area via Houston, Dallas, Tulsa and St Louis. The system, with varying diameters of 12, 28 and 24 inches, will transport gasoline and petroleum oil distillates at an initial rate of 295 000 b/d, with increases planned to 800 000 b/d.

In Europe the capacity of the South European Pipeline (SPLSE – Shell interest 18·94%) is being expanded by stages from 700 000 b/d to 1 800 000 b/d ultimately. The first stage was completed in December 1971 by putting into operation a 24-inch line from Fos, on the Mediterranean, to Lyon. In addition a 40-inch line is under construction from Fos to Strasbourg and is expected to be operational by end 1972.

In 1972 the capacity of the 40-inch Transalpine pipeline (TAL – Shell interest 15%) will be increased from 500 000 b/d to 800 000 b/d and the capacity of the 18-inch Adria–Wien pipeline (AWP – Shell interest 14·5%) will be increased from 120 000 to 150 000 b/d.

In 1971 in the Netherlands Gasunie (Shell interest 25%) was the first to lay 48-inch diameter steel pipe in Western Europe. In addition to the 172 kilometres laid in 1971 Gasunie plans to lay another 200 kilometres of 48-inch in 1972.

In the UK, in order to improve arrangements for the import of crude oil for Stanlow refinery, where tanker access is limited, plans are being developed to establish a deepwater tanker terminal on the island of Anglesey and to build from there a 75-mile pipeline to transport the crude oil to Stanlow.

Currently two 30-inch joint venture pipelines take gas from the Shell/Esso – Gas Council/Amoco group's Leman and Indefatigable fields in the North Sea to the UK coast at Bacton. To meet increased production capacity a development programme entailing the installation of a third line is under way.

In Victoria, Australia, construction of the WAG pipeline is scheduled for completion in late 1972. This 86-mile 24 inch/ 16 inch pipeline will transport Gippsland offshore crude from a terminal at Westernport Bay to refineries at Altona and Geelong. The Shell Company of Australia is supervising construction and will operate the line on behalf of itself, Esso and Mobil.

In Western Australia the 255-mile 14-inch West Australian Natural Gas (WANG) pipeline was put into operation in 1971. The line (Shell interest 14·3%) runs from the Dongara natural gas field to the Kwinana – Pinjarra industrial complex 50 miles south of Perth.

Japan is turning to pipelines to solve the problems of inland distribution of oil products due to increasing traffic congestion on the railway and the roads. The first major pipeline will be a 250-kilometre 18-inch products pipeline (Kanto Oil Pipeline – Shell interest 9%) around the east side of Tokyo Bay. Construction is scheduled to get under way in 1972.

In conjunction with an LNG export project to Japan Brunei LNG Limited is constructing a cryogenic loading lines system in Brunei; two 18-inch insulated lines are being laid on a trestle extending some three miles out to sea.

Refining (World)

Before World War II, most refineries were built in the producing areas, for example at Abadan and Curaçao. After World War II a programme of refinery expansion was called for and new plant was built in the major marketing countries, particularly those of Western Europe. Local product demand, coupled with advances in refining and transportation technology, enabled these refineries to be competitive with those in producing areas without in any way affecting product diversity.

These post-war refineries were initially all on the coast. More recently an increasing number have been built inland to serve large industrial areas, receiving their crude by pipeline from the coast.

Examples are:

the Shell refinery at Godorf, near Cologne, fed by the Rotterdam-Rhine pipeline;
the refinery at Reichstett-Vendenheim near Strasbourg, fed by the South European Pipeline;
the Shell refinery at Ingolstadt, fed by the Transalpine Pipeline; and
the refinery at Cressier, which is fed by an SEPL extension, the Jura pipeline.

There is now some tendency for this trend to be reversed and for new capacity on the continent of Europe to be concentrated at major seaports, rather than dispersed at inland locations. The major expansions in the Rotterdam area by a Shell Company, Esso, BP and Chevron are examples.

There has also been a demand for small refineries to serve local markets, particularly in the developing countries. New design techniques and resourceful engineering enable these refineries to operate both efficiently and economically, although their throughputs are small. The building of such refineries is still relatively expensive.

Computers are now being applied to many aspects of refining, particularly process research, including linear programming for refinery scheduling/economics, process and engineering design and maintenance schedules. The application of computer control to the operation of process units is showing encouraging results. Application of in-line blending has resulted in overall tankage reduction.

At the end of 1971, total refining capacity amounted to some 54 million b/d. In 1971 3·5 million b/d of new capacity went on stream.

World crude oil refining – 1971

Crude Oil Processed	million b/d	%
USA	11·2	24
Canada	1·4	3
Rest of Western Hemisphere	5·3	11
Europe	12·9	27
Africa	0·8	2
Middle East	2·3	5
Far East and Australasia	5·9	12
USSR, Eastern Europe and China	7·7	16
World Total	47·5	100

Refining (Shell)

Shell refineries processed an average of 5 022 000 b/d of crude oil during 1971.

Capital expenditure on refinery construction and improvement to meet the growth in demand and more stringent quality specifications require enormous sums of money. This requirement is increased additionally by the high rates of inflation experienced in recent years. This is illustrated by the figures shown below:

	£ million	total capital expenditure %
1967	96	21
1968	112	20
1969	165	28
1970	147	22
1971	199	25

For a complex refinery, capital costs may fall within the range of £400–640 per b/d of throughput capacity. For a 'simple' refinery, the range may lie between £250–400 per b/d. Operating costs show an almost equally wide variation.

During 1971 a total of some 100 000 b/d was added to capacity at refineries owned or partly owned by Shell companies.

Furthermore, upgrading units have been extended or added to existing refineries; e.g., some 80 000 b/d desulphurization capacity.

Refinery throughput – 1971
(Crude oil and natural gasoline processed)

	thousand b/d	%
USA	951	19
Canada	233	5
Rest of Western Hemisphere	860	17
Europe	2129	42
Africa	76	1
Middle East	87	2
Far East and Australasia	686	14
Total	5022	100

The volume of oil to be handled is growing every year and Shell companies explore many paths to acquire safe storage capacity at an economic cost. Floating-roof steel tanks up to 150 000 m³, and open pits for residue storage up to 1 000 000 m³ are in use. Underground storage caverns up to 100 000 m³ have been constructed and there is no technical limit to the cavern size. Exhausted salt cavities are also being used for oil storage.

With the use of large tankers increasing rapidly, shore facilities to accommodate these giant vessels are to be brought in line. At a number of locations single-buoy mooring berths are or will be installed, simplifying mooring operations.

The increase in refinery capacity has coincided with a growing awareness of the importance to local communities of clean air and water. Shell companies have long accepted their own responsibilities for this by applying constantly improving anti-pollution safeguards; up to 10% of the capital expenditure budget for refinery construction can be devoted to environmental conservation.

A number of Shell systems for improvements in design and operating techniques have been made available to other operators to assist them to maintain the high safety and pollution-prevention standards required both by the local authorities and the oil industry in general.

Location of refineries

There are some 74 refineries operated or under construction by Royal Dutch/Shell companies, or by companies in which there is a Shell interest. The position on 31 December 1971 is shown below.

	Atm distilling capacity	Financial participation	
	thousands b/d	%	

North America
United States

Anacortes (Washington)	88	69	Shell
Ciniza (New Mexico)	17	31	Public
Houston (Texas)	255		
Martinez (California)	100		
Norco (Louisiana)	240		
Odessa (Texas)	29		
Wilmington (California)	86		
Wood River (Illinois)	245		

Canada

Bowden (Alberta)	5	87	Shell
Montreal (Quebec)	100	13	Public
Oakville (Ontario)	40		
St Boniface (Manitoba)	27		
Sarnia (Ontario)	56		
Shellburn (British Columbia)	21		

Caribbean, Central and South America
Venezuela

Cardón	348	100
San Lorenzo	32	

Netherlands Antilles

Curaçao	360	100

Argentina

Buenos Aires	115	100

Trinidad

Point Fortin	80	100

	Atm distilling capacity	Financial participation	
	thousands b/d	%	
El Salvador			
Acajutla	13	35	Shell
		65	Esso
Guatemala			
Santo Tomás de Castilla	11	40	Shell
		60	Socal
Martinique			
Fort de France	11	24	Shell
		25	CFP
		25	ELF Union
		14·5	Esso
		11·5	Texaco
Dominican Republic			
Nigua	30	50†	Shell
		50†	Government

Europe

United Kingdom			
Ardrossan	6	100	
Heysham	39	100	
Shell Haven	200	100	
Stanlow	215	100	
Teesport	110	100	
France			
Berre l'Etang	165 ⎫	86·45	Shell
Pauillac	90 ⎬	13·55	Public
Petit-Couronne	180 ⎭		
Reichstett-Vendenheim	75	79·99	Shell
		10	ELF UIP
		5	Mobil
		5·01	Public

† Initially

	Atm distilling capacity	Financial participation	
	thousands b/d	%	
Netherlands			
Pernis	500	100	
West Germany			
Godorf	180	100	
Harburg	85	100	
Ingolstadt	55	100	
Misburg	54	50	Shell
		50	Esso
Monheim	7	100	
Italy			
La Spezia	86	100	
Rho	75	100	
Taranto	90	100	
Sweden			
Gothenburg	100	100	
Switzerland			
Cressier	50	75	Shell
		25	Gulf
Irish Republic			
Whitegate	54	24	Shell
		16	BP
		40	Esso
		20	Texaco
Denmark			
Fredericia	59	100	
Belgium			
Ghent	9	100	
Norway			
Sola	46	100	

	Atm distilling capacity	Financial participation	
	thousands b/d	%	

Africa

South Africa

Durban	84	50	Shell
		50	BP

Kenya

Mombasa	48	12·75	Shell
		12·75	BP
		12·75	Esso
		11·75	Caltex
		50	Government

Nigeria

Alese	52	25	Shell
		25	BP
		50	Government

Sudan

Port Sudan	20	50	Shell
		50	BP

Sierra Leone

Freetown	10	17·7	Shell
		6·9	BP
		11·3	Mobil
		10·8	Texaco
		3·3	AGIP
		50	Government

Ivory Coast

Abidjan	20	14·7	Shell
		10	Government
		10·2	BP
		13	CFP
		1	Esso
		18·2	Mobil
		7·9	Texaco
		25	ELF Union

H

	Atm distilling capacity	Financial participation	
	thousands b/d	%	
Senegal			
Dakar	12	11·8	Shell
		11·8	CFP
		11·8	Mobil
		11·8	Texaco
		11·8	BP
		10	BSD
		6	SAP
		24	ELF Union
		1	Esso
Malagasy Republic			
Tamatave	12	6·45	Shell
		7·5	CFP
		6·45	BP
		15	Government
		13·7	Esso
		8	SPM
		12·1	Caltex
		3·8	AGIP
		27	ELF Union
Gabon			
Port Gentil	17	11·4	Shell
		2·5	AGIP
		5	Rep Fed Cameroon
		5	Rep Centrafricaine
		5	Rep Congo Brazzaville
		5	Rep Gabonaise
		5	Rep du Tchad
		18·75	ELF Union
		18·75	CFP
		3·1	BP
		11·6	Mobil
		5·6	Texaco
		3·3	Petrofina

	Atm distilling capacity	Financial participation	
	thousands b/d	%	
Rhodesia			
Umtali*	20	20·75	Shell
		20·75	BP
		17·75	Mobil
		15·75	Caltex
		15	Aminoil
		5	KNPC
		5	Total

Middle East

	Atm distilling capacity	Financial participation	
Iran			
Abadan	430	14	Shell
		40	BP
		7	Esso
		7	Texaco
		7	Socal
		7	Mobil
		7	Gulf
		6	CFP
		5	Iricon
Turkey			
Mersin	95	27	Shell
		56	Mobil
		17	BP
Lebanon			
Tripoli	24	23·75	Shell
		23·75	CFP
		23·75	NEDC
		23·75	BP
		5	Partex
Cyprus			
Larnaca	12	25·5	Shell
		25·5	BP
		34	Mobil
		15	Petrolina

* Mothballed

	Atm distilling capacity	Financial participation	
	thousands b/d	%	

East and Australasia

Japan

Kawasaki	140	50	Shell
Niigata	42	50	Others
Yokkaichi	170	50	Shell
		25	Mitsubishi
		25	Others
Onoda	47	20	Shell
		23	Japan Line
		23	Ube Kosan
		10	Chugoku Denryoku
		7	Kogyo Bank
		17	Others

Australia

Clyde	55	100	
Geelong	92	100	

Malaysia

Lutong	60	100	
Port Dickson	31	75	Shell
		25	Public

Singapore

Pulau Bukom	250	100	

India

Bombay	76	50	Shell
		50	Burmah Oil

Philippines

Tabangao	67	75	Shell
		25	Public

Pakistan

Karachi	50	15	Shell
		12	Caltex
		15	Burmah Oil
		18	Esso
		40	Public

	Atm distilling capacity	Financial participation	
	thousands b/d	%	
New Zealand			
Whangarei	54	17·1	Shell
		31·4	Public
		19·2	Mobil
		15·1	BP
		8·6	Caltex
		8·6	Europa Oil

Explanation of abbreviations

(see also 'Some other oil and chemical companies', pages 19–48)

ELF UIP = ELF Union Industrielle des Pétroles
BSD   = Banque Sénégalaise de Développement
SAP   = Société Africaine de Pétrole
SPM   = Société de Pétrole Malgache

Demand and supply pattern

In 1971, the growth in world energy consumption outside the USSR, China and the East European countries was somewhat slower than for several years, in line with the generally reduced pace of economic growth. Overall energy demand increased by 4% over 1970 to reach 5500 million metric tons coal equivalent (72 million b/d oil equivalent). The pattern of energy consumption, however, continued to reflect the trends of recent years. Coal lost more ground to oil and natural gas, its share of total consumption suffering a further decline. Environmental considerations contributed to this situation and were also an important factor, notably with regard to public safety, in the field of nuclear power. While the share of nuclear-generated electricity in total energy supply increased, its relative importance remained small by comparison with other sources of energy. A number of existing stations were dogged by technical problems, whilst plant completions fell below planned levels. Nevertheless, despite the disappointments and delays which have beset nuclear power, there is little doubt that in the long term it will become a major source of world energy.

Petroleum fuels accounted for well over half of total energy demand in 1971. With the inclusion of the non-energy products (chemical feedstocks, lubricants, bitumen, etc), total consumption of oil products exceeded 40 million b/d, an increase of 6% over 1970. This below-trend increase reflects the rather slow growth of total energy and increasing competition from natural gas in Europe. Eastern Hemisphere oil demand continued to account for more than half of total consumption in the world outside the USSR, Eastern Europe and China.

The largest regional increase in oil demand (8%) took place in Asia and Australasia, despite a rate of growth in Japan markedly lower than for many years past. Demand in Western Europe also advanced at a much slower pace, registering an increase of only 5% over 1970. North American consumption grew by 3%, likewise below the historical trend-rate.

The supply pattern in 1971 was influenced by a number of factors apart from the slower growth in demand. In February and March the major oil producing countries exacted higher revenues from the oil companies. These amounted to an additional 30c/bbl for Middle East Gulf crudes and an additional 50–65c/bbl for African and Eastern Mediterranean crudes. The fall away in European demand after the first quarter of the year then led to a decline in ocean tanker freight rates which favoured the relatively lower priced long-haul crudes of the Middle East Gulf to the disadvantage of African crudes.

In Algeria, crude liftings were much reduced during the protracted negotiations which eventually led to nationalisation of the French oil companies' production. Finally, in December, the Libyan Government nationalised BP's production of 200 000 b/d.

In the Western Hemisphere the 'traditional' exporting refineries in the Caribbean were affected by lower US demand for high-sulphur fuel oil, which had the effect of limiting production from the main crude source – Venezuela. In contrast, US demand for low-sulphur fuel oil was higher than expected, and the additional trade was taken up by new refinery capacity in Canada and in the 'offshore' islands of the Caribbean, where the additional crudes used were largely of Eastern Hemisphere origin.

The combined effect of the lower than expected demand and the switch to Middle East Gulf crudes led to an increase over 1970 in Middle East crude oil production of 2·4 million b/d (+17%), whereas North African production declined by 0·8 million b/d (−17%) and Venezuelan by 0·25 million b/d (−4%). West African production, mainly Nigerian, increased by 0·45 million b/d (+36%).

Despite these changes in the crude oil supply pattern, the continued closure of the Suez Canal and the restrictions on North African production, the industry maintained oil supplies without interruption. A total of some 33 million b/d of oil was moved in international trade during 1971: 6% higher than in 1970. About 75% of this movement was crude oil supplied to refineries in oil consuming countries, while the balance was in the form of products representing export/import traffic in, for example, fuel oil and chemical feedstocks.

Estimated commercial energy consumption
World (excluding USSR, Eastern Europe
and China)
(million metric tons of coal equivalent)

	1962	1969	1976
Solid fuels	1150	1204	1280
Petroleum fuels§	1495	2488	4093
Natural gas*	560	914	1370
Hydro electricity†	83	108	150
Nuclear electricity	neg.	8	82
Total	3288	4722	6975

Estimated commercial energy consumption
by regions

	Solid fuels	Petroleum fuels §	Natural gas *	Hydro/ Nuclear electricity †	Total ‡
			% shares		
North America					
1962	23	45	30	2	1726
1969	21	44	33	2	2382
1976	19	45	32	4	3140
Western Europe					
1962	55	40	2	3	973
1969	33	58	5	4	1351
1976	16	67	13	4	2000

Rest of world (excluding USSR, Eastern Europe and China)

1962	36	57	4	3	589
1969	25	67	5	3	989
1976	20	72	5	3	1835

§ Includes refinery use and loss
* Includes net imports/exports of manufactured gas
† Includes net imports/exports of electrical energy
‡ Million metric tons of coal equivalent

	Solid fuels	Petroleum fuels	Natural gas	Hydro/ Nuclear electricity	Total
				% shares	

World (excluding USSR, Eastern Europe and China)

	Solid fuels	Petroleum fuels	Natural gas	Hydro/ Nuclear electricity	Total
1962	35	46	17	2	3288
1969	26	53	19	2	4722
1976	18	59	20	3	6975

Total consumption of petroleum products in representative countries
(including aviation fuels and ocean bunkers)

	1970	1971
		b/d
USA	14 007 379	14 472 257
Japan	3 887 867	4 258 884
West Germany	2 613 248	2 704 195
UK	1 972 842	1 996 828
Canada	1 408 108	1 450 353
Netherlands	707 777	711 149
Sweden	588 921	554 035
Australia	485 835	511 502
Argentina	416 520	446 109
India	365 813	404 840
South Africa	243 194	266 531
Venezuela	182 522	191 712

Estimated world oil supply pattern by zones January–December 1971

From	North America	Caribbean	South America	Europe
To				
North America	1210*	2900	5	150
Caribbean	20	1200*	10	5
South America	15	200	15*	10
Europe	25	555	2	2300
Africa	5	50	–	80
Middle East/Levant	1	1	–	5
Indian sub-continent	2	1	–	–
Far East	50	20	1	
Australasia	10	1	–	
USSR/Eastern Europe/China	–	–	–	
Totals	1338	4928	33	2584

Net imports (−)   Net exports (+)

−4124   +3059   −623   −13 355

* International intra-zonal movements
† Not available

1969 per capita consumption
(excluding aviation fuels and ocean bunkers)

	Imp gal		Imp gal
Sweden	792	UK	395
USA	767	Japan	370
Canada	748	Argentina	203
Netherlands	469	Venezuela	159
West Germany	466	South Africa	95
Australia	411	India	7

Africa	Middle East and Levant	Indian sub-continent	Far East	Austral-asia	USSR/ Eastern Europe/China	Total
						thousand b/d
460	600	–	120	10	7	5 462
340	160	–	10	–	124	1 869
115	300	–	–	–	1	656
4600	7 550	–	10	1	896	15 939
145*	635	–	7	3	69	994
20	580*	2	2	–	4	615
2	405	1*	10	–	11	432
60	4 700	10	1140*	30	23	6 037
1	295	–	75	15*	1	398
61	64	–	–	–	–†	156
5804	15 289	13	1374	59	1136	32 558
810	+14 674	–419	–4663	–339	+980	–

1971 pattern of product demand
per cent of total consumption by volume
(including aviation fuels and ocean bunkers)

	USA	UK	Western Europe ex UK	Japan	India
Gasolines	45	28	23	21	17
Kerosines	7	7	3	7	23
Gas oil/diesel fuel	19	19	33	11	28
Fuel oil	14	40	33	52	23
Others	15	6	8	9	9
	100	100	100	100	100

1971 estimated world (excluding USSR, Eastern Europe and China) consumption of petroleum products
(including aviation fuels and ocean bunkers)

	thousand b/d	thousand tons/year
Aviation gasoline	97	3 964
Motor gasoline	10 164	428 297
Aviation turbine fuels	1 767	79 486
Kerosine	1 234	55 703
Gas/diesel fuels	9 019	428 618
Fuel oil	11 594	628 735
Others	6 198	261 128
Total	40 073	1 885 931

1971 estimated world consumption of petroleum products by regions
(including aviation fuels and ocean bunkers)

	thousand b/d	thousand tons/year
North America	16 574	749 438
Caribbean and South America	2 111	100 618
Total Western Hemisphere	18 685	850 056
Western Europe	12 777	615 772
Middle East and Africa	1 961	97 376
Asia and Australasia	6 650	322 727
Total Eastern Hemisphere	21 388	10 358 75
World total	40 073	1 885 931

(excluding USSR, Eastern Europe and China)

Markets and sales (World)

Marketing embraces all the activities directly concerned with the identification and satisfaction of customer needs. It generates the funds for further investment and constitutes the last link in the chain of oil operations which starts with exploration.

Oil is a primary commodity and a main source of energy: its value is governed basically by supply and demand which in turn is influenced by technological development and the continuous improvement in the standard of living throughout the world.

Marketing and distribution involve getting oil products to the customer when and where he wants them, of the quality and in the quantities he requires them, and call for a great deal of capital investment. In 1971 the major international groups of oil companies invested a total of over $7900 million, of which more than $1790 million went into marketing facilities. During the ten years ending in 1971 these companies, Shell, Esso, Mobil, Texaco, Gulf, Socal and BP, together invested about $13 000 million in property, plant and equipment for marketing alone.

World-wide* oil consumption during 1971 was 48 million b/d, representing an increase of about 6% over 1970. 54% of all oil products sold in the world was marketed by the seven major international companies already mentioned. This, however, does not cover the whole market since there are, for example, many thousands of independent marketing companies and jobbers in the United States and about 450 in Europe.

Market situation

During the period from 1958 to 1969 the supply situation outside North America was generally one of surplus in crude availability, refinery capacity and tanker tonnage, leading to fierce competition in the markets.

The rapidly growing demand for oil and the enormous

---

* Throughout this section 'world' excludes the USSR, Eastern Europe and China

absolute growth in volume recorded year after year provided an attractive background for new entrants to the market and encouraged the expansion outside North America of a number of American companies, e.g. Standard of Indiana, Phillips Petroleum, Continental and Occidental. Many of these companies have now set up fully integrated operations outside North America, in some cases as a result of the introduction of the US import control system in 1959, which limited outlets to that country for their overseas crude oil.

The last two years have seen rapid changes in the market situation. Throughout 1970, demand for oil in the developed countries continued to grow rapidly – in fact more so than expected – leading to higher prices for products as tankers and refining capacity became fully utilised.

This boom continued into the first quarter of 1971, with consumers building up stocks of oil against a possible rupture of supplies in the event of a breakdown of the Teheran negotiations. These negotiations between the oil companies and the governments of the main oil producing countries resulted in significantly increased crude oil costs throughout the world. A combination of higher costs, high oil stocks, milder weather, and a slackening in industrial growth all impinged on oil demand at the same time, bringing growth down to low levels and resulting in a rapid fall away in market prices from the levels reached in 1970.

From mid-1971 onwards tankers were once again in surplus and refinery capacity was readily available. These conditions, coupled with a continuing surplus of crude oil, are likely to persist for at least the next year or two and to give rise to intensified competition as oil companies attempt to improve their positions in a slower growing market.

Sales of oil products by the majors

	1970	1971	increase
	thousand b/d		%
Standard (New Jersey)	5684	5587	—1·7
Royal Dutch/Shell	5246	5207	—0·7
Texaco	2917	3140	+7·6
Mobil	2145	2248	+4·8
British Petroleum	2088	2030	—2·8
Standard California	1919	2045	+6·6
Gulf	1545	1540	—0·3

Markets and sales (Shell)

Shell companies, taken as a whole, are amongst the foremost international marketers of crude oil and of a full range of petroleum products and services designed to meet the needs of customers in all classes of market.

Total sales of crude oil and products by Shell companies marketing in over 100 countries rose from an average of 5 918 000 b/d in 1970 to 6 009 000 b/d in 1971.

1971 Sales of crude oil and oil products – by regions

	thousands b/d
Crude oil	
USA and Canada	95
Other areas	707
Oil products	
USA	1299
Canada	346
Rest of Western Hemisphere	468
Europe	2087
Rest of Eastern Hemisphere	1007
Total	5207

In addition to playing a leading role internationally in the aviation and marine markets, Shell companies are continuing to expand their sales in inland markets. These are often complex and present a challenge to effective planning and implementation if the needs of diverse consumers are to be satisfied. A 'customer-orientated' approach has been adopted and the past few years have seen the general introduction in Shell companies of Class of Market organizations. Varying as a function of local market conditions, this approach basically involves organizing and allocating systematically total marketing effort to reflect the consumer pattern; this could include any or all of these typical categories: motorists, householders, farmers, construction and civil engineering contractors, a wide variety of industrial and commercial concerns as well as national and local agencies.

Shell companies net fixed assets in marketing at the end of 1971 were £1096 million and capital expenditure for the year was £218 million.

The automotive retail market

Activity in this market not only satisfies the requirements of both motor-car and owner, but also acts, through service stations round the world, as a shop window for Shell companies.

Considerable attention is paid to the design of facilities (buildings, pumps, signs, etc), to the 'aftermarket' (Shell shops, car washes, etc) and also to the quality of Shell automotive products and to the way these are advertised and promoted.

Technical service

Consumer needs are seldom confined to the supply of products. Attendant needs are quite diverse, and in the industry markets technical service features largely. For example, consumers in industry require lubricants for a wide variety of plant, and require help in the selection and rationalization of lubricants for many applications. They also value preventive maintenance schemes through which costly involuntary shut-down may be obviated.

The distribution pattern

The main products for inland distribution are manufactured in local refineries or imported from overseas into the larger oil installations on the coast. From these supply centres the products are transported in the most economical way – by sea, rail, road, or in certain instances by pipeline – through a network of smaller oil depots. Delivery is effected direct to service stations, resellers and consumers from whatever point in the distribution system achieves the lowest delivered cost to customers.

Transport costs are substantial and often account for 35% of total marketing costs; they are very much affected by rising wages and salaries and increases in the price of equipment. The distribution activity now engages highly technical and special-ised personnel, assisted to an increasing extent by computers, to deal effectively with day-to-day problems, and to plan and invest for continuing efficiency in the future. Increasing use is made of automation as a means of holding down operating costs. Some idea of the scale of the distribution activity can be obtained from the fact that, outside North America, Shell companies operate 1500 marketing installations, over 22 000 lorries, 20 000 rail tank wagons and about 450 000 dwt of coastal shipping.

I

Chemicals (World)

Features of the chemical industry are its complexity, and its relatively rapid growth and change. Starting with minerals, metals and hydrocarbons as raw materials, an enormous variety of processes is used to make many thousands of widely differing products.

Chemicals now stand second in size to engineering in the world* industrial league. In 1970 chemical manufacture represented 10 % of world industrial output (value added basis). Gross sales value amounted to $125 000 million, rather higher than the corresponding value of all petroleum products. Ownership of the industry is less concentrated than in the oil industry. The 20 largest chemical companies account for 25 % of world chemical sales, whereas the seven oil majors share 55 % of the business.

Location of the chemical industry is heavily concentrated in the industrialised areas of the world.

Shares of world chemical production – 1971

North America	45 %
Western Europe	35 %
Japan	9 %
Other areas	11 %

For many years chemical production has grown faster than industrial production.

Percentage average annual growth rates 1963–70

	All industry	Chemicals
World	6·0	9·0
North America	5·0	7·5
Western Europe	5·5	9·5
Japan	14·5	15·0
Other areas	7·5	8·0

* Throughout this section 'world' excludes the USSR, Eastern Europe and China

In 1971 the increase in demand for chemicals was below the average for the 1960s, mainly because of much slower economic growth. Much plant capacity was under-employed.

Chemicals may be divided broadly into two categories:

Inorganic chemicals, largely mineral derived, such as sulphuric acid, caustic soda, ammonia and chlorine. Most are large-volume, low-value products used in industry or in further chemical manufacture. The contribution of petroleum as a source is limited to ammonia, sulphur and carbon black.

Organic chemicals, those based on a framework of carbon atoms, combined with hydrogen and other elements. They are increasingly derived from petroleum which on economic grounds is taking over rapidly from coal and other raw materials. The organics are far more numerous and of higher value than the inorganics. Examples of their end-products are plastics, synthetic fibres, synthetic rubbers, solvents, detergents and pharmaceuticals.

World production of basic organic chemicals was about 65 million tons in 1970 compared with 20 million tons in 1960. 90% of their output is now petroleum-derived.

Production of chemicals from petroleum

The basic petroleum raw materials for the production of chemicals are:

- liquid hydrocarbon fractions (principally naphthas)
- refinery gases
- natural gas
- fuel oil and certain types of wax

Manufacture in the USA is based mainly on natural gas and refinery gases although there is a trend towards greater use of heavier feedstocks. In other areas, where there is a restricted availability of suitable natural and refinery gases, naphthas are cracked on a large scale in plants specially designed to give high yields of base chemicals such as olefins. In most areas reformate (platformate) is the prime source of aromatic base chemicals such as benzene. Feedstocks for chemicals now represent 5% of world petroleum consumption.

The original development of petroleum-based chemical manufacture in the USA has been followed by even more rapid establishment of production in Western Europe and Japan and, on a smaller scale, in many other areas.

World production of organics from petroleum has grown at an average of 15% per year to reach 59 million tons in 1970. This was distributed as follows:

	Million metric tons	
	1960	1970
World	**13·0**	**59·0**
USA	10·0	26·5
Western Europe	2·3	19·0
Japan and others	0·7	13·5

World investment in plants to make basic organic chemicals from petroleum is estimated to have reached a cumulative total of £10 000 million (at cost) in 1970.

Rapid advances in the scale and efficiency of production and severe competition led to substantial reductions in selling prices. These, combined with the recent acceleration of cost inflation world-wide, are adversely affecting profitability. Substantial price increases are required to restore profitability to a healthy level and support new investment.

Most of the leading oil companies supply petroleum feed-stocks to the chemical industry, and manufacture chemicals themselves on a large and growing scale. By 1970 they accounted for about 40% of the total investment in petroleum-based chemical plants, including their participation in numerous joint ventures with chemical companies.

Principal petroleum-derived products and uses

The following products are 90% or more derived from petroleum. Estimates are given for their world production from all sources in 1970.

Plastics and resins. 26·5 million metric tons. *Thermoplastics* include three major types, polyolefins (polyethylenes and polypropylene); polyvinyl chloride and polystyrenes. Used to manufacture an immense variety of moulded goods, packaging films, bottles, pipes, flooring, etc. *Thermosetting resins* include phenolic and amino/formaldehyde resins, alkyds, polyesters, urethanes, epoxies, etc. Used for mouldings, laminates, reinforced and insulating plastics, paints, foams, etc.

Synthetic rubbers. 4·7 million metric tons. Synthetic types account for two out of every three tons of rubber used world-wide. Used in manufacture of tyres and most other products of the rubber industry.

Synthetic fibres. 4·6 million metric tons. Synthetics represent 20% of world consumption of all fibres. Main types are polyamides (e.g. nylon), polyesters (e.g. 'Terylene', 'Dacron'), polyacrylics (e.g. 'Acrilan', 'Orlon') and polypropylene.

Synthetic detergents. Represent half of total washing and cleaning materials of all kinds.

Solvents. 15 million metric tons. Hydrocarbon and chemical solvents used primarily in the manufacture of paints and lacquers. Chemical solvents find large additional use as intermediates for other chemicals.

Agricultural chemicals. A number of pesticides (insecticides, weedkillers, etc) are partly derived from petroleum. Over 80% of world ammonia production for nitrogenous fertilizers is petroleum-derived.

Chemicals (Shell)

With sales proceeds of £581 million in 1971, Shell companies' chemical business is among the 12 largest in the world. These proceeds from chemicals represented $11\frac{1}{2}\%$ of the total business, and exceeded the chemicals sales of any other oil company. They have been growing at about 11% per year since 1961.

Chemicals proceeds – £ million		
	1961	1971
World	192	581
North America	90	216
Western Europe	68	272
Rest	34	93

The distribution of chemical sales is now approximately 37% in North America, 47% in Western Europe and 16% in remaining areas. Shell sales outside North America, like the chemical industry itself, have been growing faster than they have in North America.

Shell companies' net investment in chemicals world-wide exceeded £500 million by the end of 1971. In addition investment in a number of joint ventures in which there is a Shell interest of 50% or less is approximately £50 million. Recent capital expenditure on wholly owned chemical plants has been as follows:

	1970	1971
		£ million
North America	22	15
Europe	44	88
Rest	6	2
Total	72	105

Shell chemical manufacture is located principally in North America (fifteen locations) and in Western Europe (eight main locations). In the USA chemicals are manufactured and marketed by Shell Chemical Company and in Canada by Shell Canada. In Western Europe the wholly owned interests are in the UK (Carrington, Stanlow, Shell Haven and Ince), the Netherlands (Pernis), France (Berre) and West Germany (Godorf). There are also joint ventures in the Netherlands, West Germany, France and Spain. Outside Western Europe there are wholly owned plants in Australia and the Netherlands Antilles and minority interests in important ventures in Japan and India. A list of manufacturing locations and products is given on pages 137–42.

In over 80 countries marketing of chemicals is carried out by chemical divisions of local Shell petroleum companies. Separate chemical marketing companies have been established in West Germany, South, Central and East Africa, the Philippines, Japan, Mexico, Brazil and Venezuela. In the USA, the UK, the Netherlands, France and Australia, separate Shell chemical companies both market and manufacture. In certain areas, e.g. in Eastern Europe and the Middle East, sales are made directly from London, often with the assistance of local agents or distributors.

Shell companies manufacture and market a broad range of several hundred chemicals. Base chemicals and intermediates are made on a large and growing scale both to support Shell production of derivatives and for sale. Taken together Shell companies have the leading position in world solvent markets, and are among the leaders in detergent intermediates and other industrial chemicals. They have a leading position in epoxy resins and (including their joint ventures) are among the leaders in major thermoplastics. Shell companies have the third largest business in general-purpose synthetic rubbers. They are among the world's top three suppliers of pesticides and have several interests in fertilizers.

The marketing of chemicals requires a high level of technical expertise and is supported by technical service work carried out at laboratories. Shell companies have technical service laboratories at Carrington, Egham and Sittingbourne in the UK, at Delft in the Netherlands, at Berre in France, and at several locations in the USA, Canada, Australia and elsewhere. Comments on Shell chemical research are given in the Research section.

Recent highlights (mid-1971 to mid-1972)
Despite the currently adverse economic and chemical industry environments, plant investment is going forward in selected fields.

Base chemicals
A large olefins plant is under construction at the new site of Moerdijk in the Netherlands. Plants to manufacture xylene isomers were completed in the USA and West Germany.

Industrial chemicals and intermediates
In the USA a large vinyl chloride plant was brought into operation at Houston and another is to be built at Norco, Louisiana. New plants were completed for solvents and other industrial chemicals in the Netherlands, for detergent alcohols in the UK and for isocyanates in Belgium. Manufacture of cumene in France and phenol in the UK is due to start later this year.

Plastics, rubbers and resins
Polystyrene manufacturing capacity has been increased in the USA and the UK. Epoxy resins' capacity is being enlarged at several locations. A thermoplastic rubbers plant is to be built at Wesseling in West Germany.

Agricultural chemicals
Two new herbicides for weed control in cereals and other crops were introduced to the market. A pesticides formulation plant began operation in Iran and a pesticides centre including formulation plants and laboratories was opened at Kakegawa in Japan.

Shell chemical plants and products
1 Wholly or majority owned
2 50% Shell interest
3 Minority interest
* New capacity under construction or planned

Country	Location and principal products
Australia	*Clyde*[1] Ethylene, propylene; acetone-derived solvents, hydrocarbon solvents, toluene, xylene; epoxy resins, polypropylene *Geelong*[1] Hydrocarbon solvents, detergent alkylate; 'Shelltox' pest strips
Belgium	*Antwerp*[2] Isocyanates
Canada	*Montreal*[1] Propylene, butylenes; propylene and butylene derived solvents; epoxy resins *Sarnia*[1] Benzene, toluene, xylenes
France	*Berre*[1] (*Marseille*) Ethylene, propylene, butylenes, butadiene, higher olefins, benzene, toluene, xylenes; propylene and butylene-derived solvents, detergent alkylate, non-ionic detergents, luboil additives, cyclododecatriene; styrene-butadiene and butadiene rubbers; 'Phosdrin' insecticide, 'Vapona' pest strips *Berre*[2] Low-density polyethylene *Pauillac* Cumene*

Country	Location and principal products
India	*Bombay*[3] Ethylene, propylene, butadiene, benzene; ethylene oxide and derivatives, dichloroethane, vinyl chloride, PVC resins and compounds; propylene derived solvents, plasticiser alcohols
Iran	*Gazvin*[3] Formulated pesticides
Italy	*Rho*[1] Benzene, toluene, xylenes
Japan	*Kakegawa*[1] 'Vapona' pest strips, formulated pesticides *Kashima*[3] Ethylene, propylene, benzene, xylenes; cumene, ethyl benzene, styrene, ethylene oxide and derivatives; low-density polyethylene, polypropylene *Yokkaichi*[3] Ethylene, propylene, benzene, toluene, xylenes, ammonia; ethyl alcohol, detergent alkylate, ethyl benzene, styrene, ethylene oxides and derivatives, detergent alcohols, ethanol; low and high density polyethylenes, polypropylene, epoxy resins, acrylic esters; fertilizers
Mexico	*Atotonquillo*[3] Epoxy resins

Country	Location and principal products
	Mexico City[1] 'Vapona' pest strips
The Netherlands	*Amsterdam*[3] Fertilizers
	IJmuiden[3] Ammonia, fertilizers
	Moerdijk[1]* Ethylene, propylene, butylenes, butadiene; ethylene oxide and derivatives
	Pernis[1] Ethylene, propylene, butylenes, butadiene, isoprene, higher olefins; propylene and butylene derived solvents, hydrocarbon solvents, 'Teepol' and non-ionic detergents, ethylene oxide and derivatives, propylene oxide derivatives, allyl chloride, epichlorhydrin, glycerine, ethyl benzene, styrene, vinyl chloride, 'Versatic' acids, naphthenic acids, sulphur, polyvinyl chloride*, polypropylene, epoxy resins, 'Cardura' resins, 'VeoVa' vinyl monomers, vinyl 'Versatic' esters; styrene-butadiene and polyisoprene rubbers; insecticides, nematicides, herbicides, molluscicide
	Pernis[3] Ammonia, fertilizers
Netherlands Antilles	*Curaçao*[1] Benzene, toluene, xylenes

Country	Location and principal products
Puerto Rico	*Guayanilla Bay*[2] Cyclohexane
South Africa	*Germiston*[3] Polystyrene
Spain	*Tarragona*[3] Ethylene, propylene; propylene-derived solvents, ethylene oxide and derivatives, octanol plasticiser alcohol, acetaldehyde and acetic acid
UK	*Carrington*[1] Ethylene*, propylene*, butylenes*, butadiene*, benzene; ethyl benzene, styrene, ethylene and propylene oxides and derivatives, non-ionic detergents; low and high density polyethylenes*, polypropylene* *Ince*[1] Ammonia, fertilizers, nitric acid *Shell Haven*[1] Detergent alkylate, sulphur *Stanlow*[1] Propylene, butylenes, benzene*; propylene and butylene-derived solvents, Sulfolane, synthetic detergents, detergent alcohols, n-butanol, 2-ethyl hexanol, 'Linevol' plasticiser alcohols, phenol*, diphenylol propane, luboil additives, naphthenic acids, anti-static additive, corrosion inhibitors, sulphur, sulphuric acid; epoxy resins

Country	Location and principal products

USA

Deer Park, Houston[1] (Texas)
Ethylene, propylene, butylenes, butadiene, higher olefins, benzene, toluene, xylenes, para-xylene, ortho-xylene*; propylene and butylene-derived solvents, ethyl alcohol, phenol, allyl chloride, epichlorhydrin, glycerine, diphenylol propane (Bisphenol A), ethyl chloride, vinyl chloride, 2-ethyl hexanol, chlorine, caustic soda; epoxy resins; nematicide

Denver[1] (Colorado)
Insecticides, soil fumigant, herbicide

Dominguez[1], Wilmington (California)
Propylene, butylenes, benzene; propylene and butylene-derived solvents

Geismar[1] (Louisiana)
Ethylene oxide and derivatives, detergent alcohols and derivatives

Marietta[1] (Ohio)
Polystyrene; polyisoprene and thermoplastic rubbers

Martinez[1] (California)
Butylenes, benzene; butylene-derived solvents, luboil additives, anti-oxidants

Mobile[1] (Alabama)
Insecticides

Norco[1], (Louisiana)
Ethylene, propylene, butylenes; propylene and butylene-derived solvents, Sulfolane, vinyl chloride*, epichlorhydrin, glycerine, hydrogen peroxide; nematicide

Country	Location and principal products
	Princeton[1] (*New Jersey*) Insecticides and animal health products
	Shell Point[1] (*California*) Fertilizers, catalysts
	St Helens[1] (*Oregon*) Ammonia, fertilizers
	Ventura[1] (*California*) Ammonia, fertilizers
	Woodbury[1] (*New Jersey*) Polypropylene
West Germany	*Godorf* [1] Benzene, toluene, xylenes, xylene isomers
	Wesseling[2] (*Cologne*) Ethylene, propylene, butylenes, butadiene; ethyl benzene, styrene*; low and high density polyethylenes, polypropylene, polyisobutylene, epoxy resins

Metals (World*)

The world metals industry is dominated by steel production which, in tonnage terms, is more than 50 times larger than that of any non-ferrous metal.

Production of some principal non-ferrous metals

	World 1970 (thousand metric tons)	Average Annual Increase 1960–70
Aluminium	8066	8·3%
Copper	6140	3·9%
Zinc	3965	5·0%
Lead	3026	3·5%
Nickel	488	8·6%
Tin	188	2·0%
Magnesium	162	9·2%

Markets

The main non-ferrous metals, in particular copper and aluminium, have a wide variety of end uses in the building, transportation, electrical and packaging industries. Other metals such as chromium, nickel, molybdenum, manganese and cobalt are primarily used in steel alloys. Metals are substitutable in many uses, at least over the long term. Secondary production from recycled scrap is important in most major metals (e.g. 40% of US lead production in 1970 was from scrap).

Metal prices in the past have been subject to cyclical fluctuations whether the metal is sold on commodity exchanges, such as the London Metal Exchange, or on the basis of a published producer price as in the case of aluminium and nickel.

* Throughout this section 'world' excludes the USSR, Eastern Europe and China

Mining

There has been a trend towards large scale open pit mining in recent years, the scale of operations allowing the economic mining of lower grade deposits. In 1970, 159 mines each producing at least 3 million tons of ore per annum accounted for more than 50% of total mine output and, of these, 128 were open pit.

Metals are often associated in the same deposit, particularly permutations of copper, lead, zinc, silver and nickel. This factor, together with variations in host rocks, means that each deposit will usually involve its own metallurgical problems.

Developments in 1971

The slowing down of world economic growth caused a production over-capacity situation in most metals. As in previous cycles, this was reflected in depressed prices, despite efforts by some producers, particularly in aluminium, to cut production and finance stockbuilding. The coming on stream of new production facilities was delayed and many long term contracts, particularly between Australian producers and Japanese consumers, were renegotiated. Towards the end of the year, zinc and lead prices improved, partly due to the closing down of US smelters.

Metals (Shell)

The principal Shell interests in non-ferrous metals are held by Billiton NV which became a member of the Royal Dutch/ Shell Group of Companies in 1970. Billiton's total sales proceeds were £143·9 million in 1971, of which sales of metal accounted for £112·4 million.

Aluminium

Billiton operates one of the world's largest bauxite mines in Surinam. In 1971 its output was 2·3 million tons. It has a one-third interest in Holland Aluminium, which operates a 96 000 tons per year smelter at Delfzijl, The Netherlands, and is participating in major bauxite/alumina developments in Australia. Billiton also has an interest in a large Belgian manufacturer of semi-fabricated aluminium products, Sidal.

Zinc, tin and lead

Billiton has a zinc smelter at Budel, the Netherlands, but this will be replaced in 1973/4 by a new 150 000 ton electro-lytic plant at the same location being built in conjunction with a subsidiary of RTZ. Billiton's traditional metal, tin, which was formerly produced in Indonesia, is now produced in small quantities in South America and Africa but the main interest is a 50% stake in a joint mining and smelting venture in Thailand with Union Carbide. Billiton has secondary lead plants in the UK and the Netherlands. It also participates in joint ventures producing certain minor metals including vanadium and tungsten.

Through subsidiaries, including Montanore and Billiton van der Rijn (Amsterdam), Billiton Enthoven (London) and Braconnot (Paris), Billiton has major interests in metal trading including a seat on the London Metal Exchange.

Other Shell metal activities include two exploration companies, Shell Minerals Exploration (Pty) in Australia and Shell Delfstoffen in the Netherlands, and an electro-forming company in the UK, EHE Limited.

Research (Shell)

The responsibility of Research in Shell companies' oil and chemical operations is to provide new technology as required. Results should be available at the right time.

Research is not an isolated activity but is strongly interwoven with all Shell companies' activities. The main fields of operation are:

Exploration and production research

For exploration, geological and geophysical studies are supplemented by studies into the origin, migration and accumulation of oil and gas, and by work on fossil fauna and flora which are of importance in determining geological age and the conditions under which oil bearing sediments were formed. Improvements in geophysical – in particular seismic – techniques are considerably helping the search for oil.

For production, both on land and offshore, improvements are sought in drilling techniques and equipment and in all methods of bringing the crude to the surface as efficiently as possible. Computer and laboratory-size models simulating oil or gas reservoirs are increasingly used to solve in a reasonably short time practical problems concerning the optimum development of such reservoirs.

Oil process and product research

Research on refining methods is concerned with the development of new techniques and the improvement of existing ones to obtain from crude oil either better products or products at a lower cost.

Process research is concentrated on such physical separation methods as distillation and extraction, and on conversion processes to change the chemical structure of the compounds that make up the crude oil.

Promising findings in this type of research often require testing of the process on a pilot plant scale.

Product research is concerned with all aspects of product performance, and involves the development of products suitable for a given application. Exhaustive testing of products is necessary before they are ready for the market.

Natural gas research
The production and consumption of natural gas are growing fast. Research covers such aspects as the exploration, production, transport and storage of natural gas and its applications as a fuel or as a chemical feedstock.

Marine research
Studies on preventing corrosion, reducing hull friction, and automatic control aim at lowering the cost of transport by sea.

Research is also engaged in studies on anti-pollution procedures, fire and explosion hazards in tankers, and in the safe handling of products.

Chemical research
A considerable effort is directed to the discovery and development of new products, to the development of processes to manufacture these products economically on a commercial scale, and to the development of new processes for the manufacture of existing products; much effort is also devoted to improvements in the existing manufacturing processes, to the improvement of quality and performance of existing Shell products, and to the development of new applications of these products in this fast growing market. Research is being carried out on detergents, solvents, paints and other surface coatings, alkylene oxides, polyurethane foams, plastics, resins, elastomers, agricultural chemicals, etc, in addition to the base chemicals required to manufacture these products.

General research
General research comprises all the studies – often of a long-term nature – designed to support the above mentioned research activities or to explore new areas with a potential business interest.

Research is carried out on subjects in the engineering and

analytical fields, as well as on problems of a fundamental nature in chemistry, physics, mathematics and biology.

Apart from the foregoing activities the Research function is also engaged in:

Environmental conservation

Research effort is devoted to a wide variety of problems of environmental conservation, and application of the research results reinforces existing measures taken by Shell companies, in the course of their operations, to conserve the environment. Pollution of the sea by oil, biodegradable detergents, effluent treatment, engine exhaust emissions, sulphur in fuel oil and pesticide residues, are but a few of the areas of investigation.

Patents, licensing and trade marks

The patents, licensing and trade marks organization ensures that inventions emanating from research and technological work receive adequate international patent protection and that when plans are being made for the introduction of new or improved techniques or products, no conflicts arise with patents held by others. Where necessary, licences are negotiated in respect of such patents, or to acquire know-how from others, whilst on the other hand certain Shell patents and know-how are made available to industry through licensing.

General

Shell companies' expenditure on research and related activities amounted to £53 million in 1971. Some 6500 people of different nationalities are engaged in Shell research.

Shell companies in various countries have establishments where research and development work is being done. The major function of some of these laboratories is to serve local operating companies, but they also devote part of their effort to work in the interests of all other Shell companies.

While research support covers every aspect of Shell companies' oil and chemical operations – exploration, production, natural gas, marine, manufacturing and marketing – each laboratory concentrates on one or two of these activities.

The following table lists the principal research and development establishments by country and indicates their main activities.

Country and location	Activity
Canada Oakville Research Center	*Oil and chemical products and processes*
France Centre de Recherche Shell Française, Grand Couronne	*Oil products and processes*
Laboratoire de Recherche Chimique de Berre, Berre	*Industrial and agricultural chemicals, elastomers*
Japan Shell Kagaku Pesticide Development Center, Kakegawa	*Agricultural chemicals*
Shell Sekiyu Kabushiki Kaisha, Atsugi	*Oil products*
Netherlands Koninklijke/Shell Laboratorium, Amsterdam	*Oil and chemical products and processes, natural gas, marine, general research*
Koninklijke/Shell Exploratie en Produktie Laboratorium, Rijswijk, near The Hague	*Exploration and production*
Koninklijke/Shell Plastics Laboratorium, Delft	*Plastics, elastomers, resins*
UK Thornton Research Centre, near Chester	*Oil products, natural gas, marine, general research*

Country and location	Activity
Egham Research Laboratories	*Oil products, natural gas, industrial chemicals, resins*
Carrington Plastics Laboratory, near Manchester	*Plastics*
Woodstock Agricultural Research Centre, Sittingbourne	*Agricultural chemicals*
Milstead Laboratory of Chemical Enzymology, Sittingbourne	*Biochemistry*
Tunstall Laboratory, Sittingbourne	*Toxicology*
Sir Robert Robinson's Laboratory, Egham	*Fundamental organic chemistry*
Borden Microbiological Laboratory, Sittingbourne	*Microbiology*

USA

Bellaire Research Center Houston, Texas	*Exploration and production, corporate R&D in science and engineering*
Biological Sciences Research Center Modesto, California	*Agricultural chemicals, animal health & nutrition*
MTM Research Laboratory Wood River, Illinois	*Oil products*
MTM Research Laboratory Deer Park, Texas	*Oil processes, petrochemicals*
Shell Pipe Line Research and Development Laboratory Houston, Texas	*Oil transport and storage*

Country and location	Activity
Chemical Research Laboratory (a) Katy – Houston, Texas (b) Deer Park, Texas	*Industrial chemicals,* *petrochemicals,* *polymers*
Plastics and Resins Technical Center Woodbury, New Jersey	*Plastics and resins*
Elastomers Technical Center Torrance, California	*Elastomers*

West Germany
Produkte-, Anwendungs-und
Entwicklungs-Laboratorium,
Hamburg

Oil products

Personnel

The staff of Shell companies form an international community, representing more than 100 different nationalities.

At the end of 1971 the number of staff employed in consolidated Shell companies was 185 000 (compared with 214 000 in 1960) and the total wages and salaries bill was £579 million (compared with £288 million in 1960).

Staff of over 60 nationalities are at present working outside their own countries. Over 700 staff from overseas work in Shell offices, laboratories and refineries in the UK and the Netherlands. These figures exclude British staff in the Netherlands and Dutch staff in the UK.

Equal opportunities and encouragement are open to all who are able to assume positions of responsibility, regardless of nationality. The international yardstick never varies: the man chosen for a job outside his own country must match the ability of the best other countries can produce.

Further education and training

In some countries the Shell operating companies find it difficult to recruit their full requirements of qualified staff because of the limited educational facilities available locally. Scholarships are therefore awarded to suitable candidates to enable them to obtain further education in other countries. In general, those from Latin American countries go to the USA; candidates from other parts of the world go mainly to universities and technical colleges in the UK or the Netherlands.

In addition to the undergraduate awards, a number of postgraduate scholarships are granted to enable graduates from local universities to go abroad to read for a higher degree, and thus have the opportunity to widen their experience at the same time. During 1970–1 there were over 100 overseas students studying in the UK on Shell scholarships. The majority were from Nigeria, but among other countries represented were Australia, Brunei, Canada, Kenya, Libya,

Malaysia, Sabah, Sarawak, Sudan and Turkey. Students on Shell scholarships studying in the USA were from Australia, Japan, Nigeria and Venezuela.

Formal training plays an important part in the career development of staff in all Shell companies. The courses cover a very wide range; some are designed to provide knowledge and develop particular skills relevant to different aspects of the oil and chemical industries; others describe management techniques and develop manager skills. Courses may be held in countries where the companies operate, at regional training centres, or at training centres in the UK and the Netherlands. Shell staff from almost every country in the world attended training courses in the UK and the Netherlands in 1971.

Useful conversions

1 barrel	35 imperial gallons (approx)
	42 US gallons
	159 litres (approx)
	0·159 cubic metres (approx)
1 barrel crude oil a day	50–55 metric tons per annum according to the specific gravity of the crude oil
1 metric ton	2204·6 lb
	1000 kg
	7·3 barrels (approx) of crude oil

1 million barrels oil per day (b/d)
equals 50 million metric tons oil per annum (approx)
   or 77 million metric tons coal equivalent per annum (approx)
   or 5000 million (5×10^9) ft^3 natural gas/day (approx)

1 million metric tons oil per annum
equals 1·6 million metric tons coal equivalent per annum
     (approx)
   or 20 thousand barrels per day oil (approx)
   or 100 million ft^3 natural gas/day (approx)

1 million metric tons coal equivalent per annum
equals 13 thousand barrels per day oil equivalent (approx)

Natural gas units of measurement
(*see* page 80)

Linear measures

1 in (inch)	0·0254 m (metre) exact
1 ft (foot)	12 in
	0·333 yd
	0·3048 m exact
1 yd (yard)	36 in
	3 ft
	0·9144 m exact
1 m (metre)	39·37 in
	3·281 ft
	1·094 yd
	0·001 km
1 km (kilometre)	1000 m
	0·6214 mile exact
	0·54 nautical mile
1 mile	1760 yd
	1·609 km
1 nautical mile (UK)	6080 ft
	1·8532 km
	1·1515 miles

Square measures

1 ft^2 (square foot)	0·09290 sq metre
1 yd^2	9 sq feet
	0·83613 sq metre
1 m^2	10·764 sq feet
	1·196 sq yards
1 acre	4840 sq yards
	0·40469 ha
1 ha (hectare)	0·01 sq km
	2·471 acres
1 km^2	100 ha
	0·38610 sq mile
1 mile^2	2·590 sq km

Cubic measures

1 ft³ (cubic foot)	0·028317 cubic metre
	28·317 litres
	0·178 barrel
	7·4805 US gallon
	6·2288 imp gallon
1 imp pint	0·56826 litre*
1 litre*	1·760 imp pints
	0·220 imp gallon
	0·264 US gallon
	0·0063 barrel
1 US gallon	3·785 litres*
	0·8327 imp gallon
	0·0238 barrel
1 imp gallon	4·5461 litres*
	1·2009 US gallon
	0·029 barrel
1 m³	219·97 imp gallon
	264·17 US gallon
	6·290 barrels
1 gross ton or register ton (BRT)	100 cubic feet
	2·83 cubic metres

Weights

1 oz	28·350 grammes
1 lb	0·453592 kg
1 kg	2·20462 lb
1 quintal	220·5 lb
	100 kg
1 cwt	50·802 kg
	112 lb
1 metric ton (tonne)	0·98421 long ton
	1·10231 short ton
	2204·6 lb
1 English or long ton	1·01605 metric ton
	1·12 short ton
1 short ton	0·892857 long ton
	0·907185 metric ton
	2000 lb

* According to the definition (=cubic decimetre) adopted by the Conférence Générale des Poids et Mesures in 1964. The 1901 litre (=1·000028 dm³) is still legal in the UK.

Temperature

Fahrenheit/Centigrade

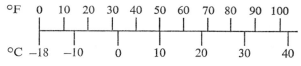

°F $\quad$ 0 $\quad$ 10 $\quad$ 20 $\quad$ 30 $\quad$ 40 $\quad$ 50 $\quad$ 60 $\quad$ 70 $\quad$ 80 $\quad$ 90 $\quad$ 100

°C $\quad$ −18 $\quad$ −10 $\quad$ 0 $\quad$ 10 $\quad$ 20 $\quad$ 30 $\quad$ 40

$°C = \frac{5}{9}(°F—32°)$
$°F = (\frac{9}{5} \times °C) + 32°$

Approximate conversion factors*

| | To convert into | | | | | | |
---	Long tons	Metric tons	Short tons	Barrels	Kilo-litres (m³)	1000 gallons (imp)	1000 gallons (US)
	Multiply by						
Long tons	1	1·016	1·120	7·42	1·18	0·260	0·312
Metric tons	0·984	1	1·102	7·30	1·16	0·255	0·306
Short tons	0·893	0·907	1	6·63	1·05	0·231	0·277
Barrels	0·135	0·137	0·151	1	0·159	0·035	0·042
Kilolitres (m³)	0·849	0·863	0·951	6·29	1	0·220	0·264
1000 gal (imp)	3·86	3·92	4·32	28·6	4·55	1	1·20
1000 gal (US)	3·21	3·26	3·61	23·8	3·79	0·83	1

* Weight/volume conversions are based on world average gravity crude oil and are accurate to within about 10%

Crude oil and products

	Barrels to long tons	Long tons to barrels	Barrels/day to tons/year	Tons/year to barrels/day
To convert	Multiply by			
Crude oil*	0·135	7·42	49·2	0·0203
Motor spirit	0·116	8·60	42·4	0·0236
Kerosine	0·127	7·90	46·2	0·0216
Gas/diesel	0·132	7·60	48·0	0·0208
Fuel oil	0·148	6·80	53·7	0·0186

* Based on world average gravity

Système International d'Unités

The metric system that is being adopted in the United Kingdom is known as the SI system of units (Système International d'Unités). It is already being legally adopted by some 25 countries and is now recognized as the one truly international system.

There are six primary units:

Quantity	Unit	Symbol
length	metre	m
mass	kilogram	kg
time	second	s
electric current	ampere	A
temperature	kelvin	K
luminous intensity	candela	cd

In addition, there are more than 20 supplementary and derived units.

Capacity is measured in cubic metres or, for smaller quantities, cubic decimetres (dm^3) but it is expected that the word litre will continue to be widely used in industry and for domestic transactions (1000 litres = 1 cubic metre).

The unit of mass is the kilogram, but in some of their dealings Shell companies will use the tonne (metric ton) which equals 1000 kg.

Despite the use of the kelvin for scientific calculations, temperatures will generally be expressed in degrees Celsius (°C), a term identical with and replacing the more familiar degrees Centigrade.

One of the advantages of SI is that there is only one name for each basic unit, with common multiples or sub-multiples for all units. Some of the prefixes used are:

Prefix	Symbol	Example
tera (a million million times)	T	terajoule (TJ)
giga (a thousand million times)	G	gigawatt (GW)
mega (a million times)	M	megawatt (MW)
kilo (a thousand times)	k	kilometre (km)
hecto (a hundred times)	h	hectobar (hb)
deca (ten times)	da	decalitre (dal)
deci (a tenth part of)	d	decimetre (dm)

centi (a hundredth part of)	c	centimetre (cm)
milli (a thousandth part of)	m	milligramme (mg)
micro (a millionth part of)	μ	microsecond (μs)

For example, the basic unit of length is the metre, a thousand metres is one kilometre, a hundredth part of a metre is one centimetre, and a thousandth part of a metre is one millimetre.

The use of the prefixes hecto, deca, deci and centi is to be discouraged and should not be extended to applications not already in common use, such as the centimetre.

It has been the practice in the oil and gas industries to use the abbreviations M, MM and T (Mcf/d, MMcf/d, Tb/d) to indicate thousand, million and thousand, respectively; MMT is also used for 'million metric tons'. With the adoption of SI, such uses of these abbreviations are to be discouraged.

For a more complete explanation of SI, see ISO Recommendation R 1000, published by the International Organization for Standardization. Shell companies may also refer to publication MOR 484, by Shell International Petroleum Company Limited.

Printed in England by Tonbridge Printers Ltd   6357/12M/7.72